DECE

DETECTION

DECEPTION
DETECTION

WINNING THE POLYGRAPH GAME

CHARLES CLIFTON

PALADIN PRESS
BOULDER, COLORADO

Deception Detection:
Winning the Polygraph Game
by Charles Clifton

Copyright © 1991 by Charles Clifton
ISBN 0-87364-621-5
Printed in the United States of America

Published by Paladin Press, a division of
Paladin Enterprises, Inc., P.O. Box 1307,
Boulder, Colorado 80306, USA.
(303) 443-7250

Direct inquires and/or orders to the above address.

CONTENTS

ACKNOWLEDGMENTS

The author wishes to thank Andee, Paul, and Bev for their help and friendship during the good and the bad times, and Adam for supplying the motivation.

CHAPTER ONE

POLYGRAPH HISTORY

LIE DETECTION THROUGH THE AGES

Why do people lie? There are, of course, a variety of answers to this question. At times we may lie in order to stay out of trouble. ("I swear I didn't cheat on that math test!") We may lie just to be polite. ("Oh, thank you for the lovely birthday present! I've always wanted a Day-Glo on black velvet painting of *The Last Supper*. Now I've just got to find a place to put it.") Sometimes we lie just to avoid a confrontation and save face. ("The check is in the mail.")

Basically, though, we lie because we are human. Situations that demand an immediate course of action are always confronting us. The small child, for example, is caught with his hand in the cookie jar after being told not to do so repeatedly. In a split second, he must decide whether to confess

1

and suffer the consequences (perhaps a spanking), or to tell a lie and extricate himself from his dilemma. ("But Daddy, I was getting this cookie for you!") Similarly, adults will resort to lying when we believe it will serve our best interests. How many of us can say that we have never fibbed about a nonexistent "previous engagement" in order to get out of an invitation to what will undoubtedly be the world's most boring dinner party?

Because of this seemingly natural predisposition we have toward lying, there have been those among us who have attempted to develop elaborate systems and electronic gadgets to "cut through all the bull" and "scientifically" determine whether an individual is really telling the truth. Perhaps the first recorded instance of an individual actively seeking to detect the truth among his contemporaries was Diogenes of Sinope (412?-323 B.C.), who searched all of Athens with a lighted lamp (even in broad daylight) to find a good and honest man. It is not known whether he ever found one, but he seems to have set the precedent for future generations to try their hands at distinguishing the honest from the dishonest.

The ancient Hindus devised a rather ingenuous method for lie detection based upon a physiological principle. Guilt or innocence was determined with a bowl of rice. The suspect was required to chew on a mouthful of rice and then spit it out. The Hindus theorized that a guilty individual, being more fearful of the test, would suffer from a dry mouth. Consequently, he would be unable to spit out the rice because it would stick to his tongue and mouth. An innocent person, on the other hand, would have no trouble in spitting out the rice because he would not have a guilty conscience.

A variation of this technique was used by the Roman Catholic Church during the Inquisition to test clergy for supposed transgressions. The cleric was forced to chew on bread and cheese to see whether he could swallow it. Perhaps the most gruesome of these "saliva" tests was devised by the Arab Bedouins of the Middle Eastern and North African deserts. In their version, conflicting witnesses each had to lick a hot iron; the one whose tongue was burned was thought to be lying.

Other early forms of lie detection were similarly based on differing types of physiological phenomena. Liars were regularly "exposed" by the frequency or amount of their perspiration, the quickness of their pulse, or the degree to which they blushed (or failed to blush) when accused of a crime. And if these methods did not work, there was always the rack, the drowning chair, and a variety of other tortures or trials by ordeal. These methods were considered acceptable and reliable in their day, but an unpleasant drawback was that innocent victims tended to die or be physically disabled in the process of being tried.

W.M. Marston

William Moulton Marston is probably the man most qualified to carry the title "father of modern-day polygraphy," for it was Marston who believed he had found a specific physiological response emitted during the act of lying. Although this claim is constantly challenged and hotly debated today, Marston, in his early excitement, proclaimed that the "long, futile search" for an empirical method of detecting deception was finally over. He publicized his new device far and wide, and possibly was the first individual to use the phrase "lie detector."

He claimed that with the lie detector, he could "read hidden thoughts like print on a page." But there were those who argued that some of Marston's uses for the polygraph were trivializing the industry. One such stunt involved using the polygraph as a marriage counselor by comparing a wife's responses first to a kiss by her husband and then to a kiss by a total stranger. It was only a matter of time before mainstream polygraphers began to openly attack Marston and his views in order to discredit him. The attacks must have worked because Marston faded from the polygraph scene and found other outlets for his creativity. Today, he is best remembered as the creator (under the name Charles Moulton) of the comic book character "Wonder Woman," a heroine who could compel people to tell the truth by lassoing them with her magical golden lariat.

John Larson

John Larson is a noteworthy individual in the history of polygraphy because, despite a tremendous initial success, he always maintained a healthy skepticism with regard to the machine and its supposed powers. As a police officer, Larson was aware of Marston's findings and their possible impact on police interrogations. It is believed that Larson thought of the polygraph as a humane form of interrogation that could be used as a favorable alternative to the all-too-common practice of beating a confession out of a suspect.

While conducting experiments on changes in blood pressure and respiration during questioning, Larson had the opportunity to put his technical skill to a practical test. A local store was suffering from shoplifting. The shopkeeper believed he knew the dormitory where the shoplifter resided but could offer no further assistance. After assembling a series of questions relevant to the crime, along with some neutral, or irrelevant, questions (soon to be called the R/I test—see Chapter 4), Larson interrogated every resident of the dormitory and singled out one girl whose responses to the relevant questions were more pronounced than those of the others. Intimidated by this unpleasant turn of events, the girl signed a full confession to the crimes, and the polygraph became indelibly marked in the annals of police history.

Though encouraged by this success, Larson remained skeptical. He differed from Marston (and most other polygraphers of the day) in that he did not believe there was any such thing as a characteristic "lie response." He was also enough of a scientist (he later became a forensic psychiatrist) to realize that the machine, as well as his own interpretations, could be plagued by a variety of errors. For that reason, he cautioned against ever using polygraph testimony as the sole source of evidence in a criminal trial. Larson was indeed ahead of his time, and it is unfortunate that most polygraphers today do not share his skeptical views.

John E. Reid

John E. Reid had a profound impact on the development of polygraph examinations, and today his is one of the biggest names in the commercial polygraph industry. He has his own company, John E. Reid and Associates, and the Reid College of Detection of Deception is named after him. He also coauthored the standard textbook for polygraph training and developed the idea of a "control" question and the control question technique (see Chapter 4).

In 1947, Reid published a paper in which he attacked the R/I test as being too imprecise. Reid (and others) had come to the conclusion that such questions as, "Did you murder John Smith last night?" or "Did you steal the five hundred dollars from petty cash?" were emotionally disturbing to the innocent and guilty alike. To counter these effects, Reid proposed a series of control questions to be interspersed throughout the test. These were designed to elicit strong responses from everybody and could be as simple as, "Have you ever stolen anything in your life?"

Although simplistic in nature, control questions served the valuable purpose of getting people to lie for the record. Reid argued that everyone would be guilty of some minor transgressions of the law in their lives, but they would be afraid to admit to them during a polygraph exam because they would fear that it might affect their credibility or be the cause for some future action to be taken against them. Reid wanted to put this fear to use, so he made the assumption that most, if not all, individuals being tested would lie on these control questions. Their fearful responses to these questions could then be compared to their responses to the relevant questions. If a person is innocent of the crime under consideration, the theory goes, he or she will have a stronger pattern of responses to the control questions. If, on the other hand, the individual is guilty of the crime under consideration, he or she will show a stronger pattern of responses to the relevant questions.

The inclusion of this pseudocontrol has done more to enhance the credibility of the polygraph than any other "advance," but the technique is still flawed. As we shall see later, there are still serious questions about a polygraph exam's reliability and validity.

Reid's other contribution to polygraph examinations was the clinical lie test, which is structured around the concept of overt behavioral symptoms, or body language. One set of symptoms is supposed to be exhibited only when a suspect is being deceptive during an examination; another set of symptoms is indicative of how a nondeceptive suspect behaves. These behavioral symptoms have been exhaustively catalogued into two surprisingly long lists and form a branch of lie detection known as kinesiology, or applied kinesics.

Applied kinesics sounds impressive, but the idea that you can detect whether a person is lying based on his or her body language is discredited by the vast majority of psychologists as well as by a good portion of today's practicing polygraphers. Don't, however, be lulled into a false sense of security—many polygraphers still use these lists as evidence that a person may be trying to be deceptive. Some of the behaviors that have been listed as indicating deception are: crossing your arms or legs, shuffling your feet, tapping your fingers, denying an accusation and immediately looking away, hesitating too long before denying an accusation, arriving late for the scheduled exam (this is a biggie and will weigh heavily against you), or leaving the examination room in a hurry once the examination is complete. All these responses are said to indicate deceptiveness, but any examiner who relies on this is opening himself up to a wave of criticism (and possibly even lawsuits) if he cannot prove the validity of these totally subjective interpretations. For example, I might think a three-second pause before answering a question is indicative of deception, but you might think seven seconds is necessary before we can really be sure that a suspect is lying. Who's right? Well, of course, neither of us is right because there are no overt behaviors that reliably signal deception. Unfortunately, a substantial number of polygraphers working today are basing their decisions on just this sort of evidence.

Cleve Backster

No history of the polygraph examination would be complete without mentioning Cleve Backster. Like Reid, he has his own school for training polygraphers, as well as a thriving commercial polygraph enterprise. Backster's approach, however, differs from Reid's on a major philosophical point: Reid's examiners are trained to use a "global" scoring technique that takes behavioral symptoms (kinesiology), "background," and other extraneous bits of information into consideration, while Backster's examiners are trained to base their decisions entirely on the data contained in the polygraph charts. Backster is also credited with initiating a numerical scoring procedure for polygraph charts. This greatly increases the reliability of the polygraph exam because it allows similarly trained examiners to reach the same conclusions about an individual chart when that chart is scored independently. In other words, if you take ten Backster-trained examiners, put them in ten separate rooms, and give them ten copies of the same individual's chart, all ten should come up with about the same numerical score and, therefore, the same conclusion about that individual's deceptiveness or truthfulness.

The scoring innovations and reliance solely on the polygraph chart are certainly points in Backster's favor, but he has also conducted some research that many serious scientists consider laughably amateurish. In the 1970s, for example, Backster wondered what would happen if a plant was hooked up to the polygraph instrument. Now, obviously, a plant has no heartbeat, nor does it "breathe" in a way that could be readily picked up by the polygraph machine's rubber respiration tubes. A plant leaf does, however, have a relatively flat surface, so Backster attached the Galvanic Skin Response (GSR) leads from the machine to the surface of the leaf. Imagine his surprise when he observed polygraph tracings on the GSR channel that were similar to human responses! As the experiment progressed, Backster actually believed that the plant might somehow be reading his mind and responding. He would demonstrate this phenomenon by standing next to the plant and thinking about cutting off part of its stem. At times, the plant would "respond" with pronounced peaks on the polygraph chart—sort of a silent cry for mercy? Unfortunately, no one has been able to duplicate this feat, and it seems fairly likely that Backster's unique responses had more to do with a poor experimental design or malfunctioning equipment than with some sort of psychic ability on the part of the plant.

LIE DETECTION TODAY

Diogenes probably never dreamed what a can of worms he was opening up when he roamed the streets of Athens with his lamp in search of an honest man. The search continues in earnest today, but the modern Diogenes gets paid for his services (some polygraphers make fifty thousand to sixty thousand dollars a year), and his "lamp" can cost upwards of five thousand dollars. Some other statistics that may surprise you about the current state of polygraphy in America are:

* One million to four million private citizens submit to a polygraph exam each year.
* 20 percent of the Fortune 500 companies and 25 percent of all other major companies use polygraph exams for screening purposes or for investigations into specific cases of theft.
* Polygraph exams are most commonly used by banks, drug companies, department stores, fast-food emporiums, discount houses, and electronics firms.
* Any business that has a large cash flow and high employee turnover is a prime prospect for a polygraph examiner.
* Testing of federal government workers has tripled in the last ten years from seven thousand to twenty-three thousand.
* Of the twenty-three thousand federal employees tested, 90 percent were being tested in criminal investigations.
* The American Polygraph Association has about three thousand members, but there are an estimated ten thousand polygraph examiners practicing today.

* Only half the states require polygraph examiners to be licensed.

* A typical polygraph exam can cost from $30 to $150 a session, and some sessions take less than twenty minutes to complete.

* A polygraph machine can range in price from $200 for a simple (GSR) recorder to $5,000 for a full-blown five-channel continuous tracking "Diplomat" or "Fact Finder" machine.

* One Atlanta, Georgia, company has cut costs to the bone by offering a most unique service: lie detection over the phone!

Indeed, polygraph examinations are big business. Some of you may be thinking, "Well, in a country of 250 million people, 4 million exams a year is really not that high a number." But you probably don't know any of the horror stories associated with them. In Chapter 2, you'll find out how ordinary, law-abiding citizens have been harassed, intimidated, coerced, and brutalized by "professional" examiners and why millions of innocent Americans are scared to death of polygraph examinations.

CHAPTER TWO

WHY BE CONCERNED ABOUT POLYGRAPH TESTS?

"Involuntary submission to a 'lie detector' test, upon pain of dismissal from employment, can constitute a tortious invasion of personal privacy, and . . . can amount to the intentional infliction of emotional distress, in contravention of the common law of North Carolina."

—Superior Court of North Carolina Restraining Order, 1979

Richard Nixon once said, "Listen, I don't know anything about polygraphs, and I don't know how accurate they are, but I know they'll scare the hell out of people." This fear is the greatest source of a polygrapher's power. An experienced examiner can easily manipulate a nervous and uninformed individual into believing just about anything.

What's worse, an experienced examiner can often extract personal and confidential information from an individual—information that would never be volunteered under different circumstances. The following set of questions, for example, were extracted from a lesson plan for the "Polygraph Examiner Training Course" taught at the U.S. Army Military Police School at Fort McClellan, Alabama. They train all federally employed polygraph examiners except those in CIA. This lesson plan was used from February 1984 until November 1985, when it was discontinued because some of the questions were deemed unacceptable by the General Accounting Office.

What do you think about the following questions? More specifically, would you cooperate with the examiner if, during a "personnel screening," he asked you the following:

* Do you have any friends who live in a foreign country?
* Do you have any foreign pen pals?
* Have you ever had a mental breakdown?
* Have you ever been confined to a rest home?
* Are you a name dropper?
* Have you ever belonged to a hobby group?
* While under the influence of alcohol, have you ever done anything you are ashamed of?
* Have you ever owed a bar bill?
* Have you ever assisted in the commission of an immoral act?
* Do you desire to engage in unnatural sex acts?
* Do you desire to continue engaging in unnatural sex acts?
* Have you ever engaged in sex acts with animals?
* Have you ever received sexual stimulation in a crowded area?
* Do you receive sexual satisfaction through means other than bodily contact?

These questions are no longer used, but there are still plenty of reasons to fear a polygraph exam. A number of employers in the early 1980s stopped checking the references supplied on employment applications because they believed it took too much of their time and was just not worth the trouble. Instead, they turned to the polygraph exam because it was quick, simple, and (for larger corporations) relatively cheap.

This practice was dealt a major blow in 1988, when Ronald Reagan signed the Polygraph Protection Act into law. There are now only a limited number of companies, plus the federal government, that can legally require polygraph exams as a condition of employment. This is not to say that the problems associated with using a polygraph for screening purposes have gone away—quite the contrary. There are still tens of thousands of hiring decisions made each year based on a series of scribblings obtained from a nameless, faceless machine.

Actually, it is not the machine that declares guilt or innocence, and that leads us to yet another problem: the woefully inadequate training given to polygraph examiners. I don't know about you, but I would rather not have my chances for employment controlled by someone who may have as little as six weeks of training (the average barber or hair stylist, by the way, must undergo nine months of training).

These criticisms are minor, however, compared to the charges of ineptitude and lack of professionalism that have been leveled against some polygraphers. If you think that you have nothing to worry about by taking a polygraph exam because you have never done anything criminal in nature, then you are sadly mistaken. Many of the people you are about to meet also believed they had nothing to fear because they were innocent. They quickly realized that "innocence" can be a relative term, and anyone, no matter how honest, can one day become a victim of false charges or unsubstantiated accusations dealt out by an overzealous polygraph examiner.

INNOCENT UNTIL PROVEN GUILTY?

John Tillson was a civilian budget analyst working for the U.S. Department of Defense (DOD). Because of his position, he was present at a variety of upper-level DOD meetings during which budget proposals were formulated and discussed. In January 1982, he attended a meeting that would change his life forever.

It all began with a fairly typical meeting of the Defense Resources Board (DRB). The board, composed of several assistant secretaries of defense as well as senior Pentagon officials, met to discuss President Reagan's defense budget. As the meeting progressed, the board soon realized that Reagan's proposed arms spending plans would exceed the defense department's budget by a whopping seven hundred billion dollars.

Understandably, the DOD did not want this explosive information to reach an already distrustful and economically jaded American public. Unfortunately, it did. The *Washington Post* somehow obtained this information from one of the participants at the DRB meeting and ran the story on the front page. Senior DOD officials were outraged and ordered polygraph examinations for everyone who had attended that meeting, including the joint chiefs-of-staff and then Deputy Secretary of Defense Frank Carlucci. Everyone at the meeting passed the lie detector tests except one man—John Tillson. A second polygraph test was given, and then a third, but Tillson failed all three times. Convinced that they had found the source of the leak, the DOD was ready to take action. Tillson, understandably shaken, pleaded his innocence. He was a West Point graduate and a Vietnam veteran, and he swore that he had not told anything to anyone after the DRB meeting had adjourned. The most he would admit to, after exhaustive interrogation, was the possibility that he had spoken with some unauthorized individuals *before* the meeting took place, but he steadfastly denied talking to anyone after the meeting.

Pentagon officials remained unconvinced until they received a letter from the *Post* reporter clearing Tillson.

Although the reporter would not reveal the true source, he did confirm that Tillson was in no way involved. Due to a lack of any other substantial evidence against Tillson, the DOD grudgingly decided not to fire him.

HOW CONTROL QUESTIONS CAN WORK AGAINST YOU

Control questions can mean different things to different people. Polygraph examiners generally assume that everyone lies on control questions because we have all committed some minor indiscretion during our lives. The theory is that innocent people will show greater emotional reactions to these questions than to questions that are directly relevant to the crime under investigation. Unfortunately, it doesn't always work that way, as the following two cases point out.

In one instance, a small-town bank discovered that four thousand dollars was missing from the vault. All the bank's employees were summarily tested, including a woman with twenty years seniority who had never been accused of anything like this in her life.

As the equipment was strapped on, she could feel her anxiety level rising. When they asked her "Did you take the four thousand dollars," her anxiety peaked—she experienced a momentary disruption of her respiration, and her heart pounded in her chest. The control questions also resulted in elevated responses, but none were so extreme as those associated with the relevant questions having to do with the actual theft. Unfortunately for her, "innocent" individuals are not supposed to react this way, and she was fired on the spot. She had not taken the money, but a polygraph examiner assumed that she had, simply because she did not respond as strongly to the control questions as she had to the relevant questions.

In another case, a woman was raped in her apartment by an unknown intruder. Not only did the intruder penetrate his victim vaginally and orally, but, among other perversities, he shaved off her pubic hair. She reported all of this to the police, and instead of comforting her, they further prolonged her ordeal. Apparently, the local sheriff had "read somewhere" that shaving off the pubic hair was a telltale sign of a lesbian rape. He asked the woman to submit to a polygraph examination so that they might determine whether the assailant was male or female. Although the woman was outraged over the assumption that the rapist might be a woman, she reluctantly submitted to the exam. Failure to do so, she reasoned, would impede the investigation because the sheriff would continue to believe that the attacker was a woman. Despite her misgivings about polygraph exams in general, the woman believed that the examiner would have to confirm her contention that the rapist was male. How could he possibly find otherwise? As you may have already guessed, this confirmation would not be forthcoming.

A problem arose when the Backster-trained examiner used, "Between the ages of eighteen and twenty-five, did you ever have sex with a woman?" as a control question. Apparently, this examiner had also "read somewhere" that every thirtyish divorcée living alone with her ten-year-old child has had at least one homosexual experience after the age of eighteen. When the woman answered "no" to this question, the examiner had to assume that this was a lie because of the way the test works. And because her responses to this control question were lower than the responses elicited from the relevant questions, the examiner had to assume that the woman was lying about the intruder being a man. Despite her protests, this was the "expert opinion" he put forth in his final report. The male rapist, consequently, had ample time to lose himself while the police department was busily searching for a lesbian rapist.

CAN A MACHINE BE FOOLED?

This is a case with an ironic twist. Usually, private citizens are the ones who suffer at the hands of police officers or other polygraph "experts." However, John K. is a deputy sheriff in Minnesota, and he had a crafty prison inmate turn the tables on him.

It all began when the inmate retrieved a hunting knife and loaded gun from his cell and gave them to a visiting federal marshal. The inmate explained that he had bribed a guard to smuggle the weapons in so that he could escape, but that he had since had a change of heart and no longer wanted to make the attempt. The federal marshal believed the inmate's story and asked which guard had supplied him with the weapons. Without batting an eye, the inmate replied that John K. had smuggled in the weapons.

This accusation resulted in polygraph examinations for both the inmate and John K. The inmate passed with flying colors; John K. flunked. Had John K. really smuggled weapons to an inmate? The Minnesota Bureau of Criminal Apprehension (they administered the polygraph) was satisfied that he had.

John's commanding officer (a sheriff) was skeptical, however, because of a letter he had received recently from a local merchant, praising John's actions. The letter told how John had gone to this merchant to buy a gift for his son, when through some sort of mix-up, the present was put in a bag containing the store's receipts, charge slips, and several hundred dollars in cash. John noticed the error when he got home, and he called the merchant immediately to tell him that the store's money was safe and would be returned when he drove to work the next morning. The sheriff realized that this story and the charges currently leveled against his deputy did not match up. Why would a man accept bribes one day and return several hundred dollars in cash the next? He began to look for other possibilities, and his thoughts turned to the inmate.

Could the inmate have lied? And if so, what had been his motive? The answer became clear when the inmate escaped from a less secure facility. Apparently, the inmate had carried out the entire ruse so that he would be transferred to a much less secure institution. This ingenious plan was verified by the inmate shortly after his recapture, when he told investigators that John K. had merely been an unwitting player in the grand scheme. In other words, the sheriff had been right, and the Minnesota Bureau of Criminal Apprehension had been wrong; the inmate had lied during his polygraph exam and been labeled truthful, and John had told the truth during his exam and had been labeled deceptive.

Do you still think you have nothing to be afraid of?

FACT: In Ohio, a man accused of murder flunked two polygraph exams given by different examiners. After being tried, convicted, and sentenced, other individuals confessed to the crime.

FACT: A North Carolina man accused of murdering his wife failed a polygraph exam, and the police were ready to file formal charges against him when she returned home from an unannounced trip.

FACT: In California, a supermarket cashier was accused of giving her mother unauthorized discounts. A polygraph exam confirmed the store's allegations, but the cashier had an airtight alibi: her mother had been dead for five years. Apparently, a combination of shock and grief had colored the girl's responses.

These examples show how things can go wrong even when polygraphers follow all the rules. More disturbing, however, are those cases in which police or unscrupulous private examiners coerce, threaten, and intimidate innocent individuals.

POLICE INTIMIDATION AND OTHER ABUSES

David Lykken, probably the most outspoken critic of polygraph examinations, has said that the Peter Reily case should be read by every polygrapher, prosecutor, and juror in cases where repudiated confessions figure into the evidence. You may already know about this case from the best-selling 1976 book, *A Death in Canaan*, by Joan Barthel (a movie has also been made).

The facts are as follows. Eighteen-year-old Peter Reily returned home late one evening to find the grossly mutilated body of his mother. The police were notified immediately and, upon arriving at the house, ushered Reily to the backseat of a patrol car. There, he waited for three hours while police conducted their preliminary investigation. What Peter didn't know was that the police were already forming strong suspicions about him—suspicions they hoped to confirm through a polygraph examination.

Early the next morning, Peter, having had only two or three hours of sleep the night before, consented and was hooked up to a polygraph instrument. Not surprisingly, he reacted strongly to questions such as, "Did you hurt your mother last night?" (I think most of us would react strongly to questions about our parents if we had found their mutilated bodies less than eighteen hours ago!) Although the young man initially denied all the police's allegations, the lack of sleep and general state of shock began to take its toll. He became confused and frightened and slowly began to tell the police examiners what he thought they wanted to hear.

Because the several-hour examination was tape recorded, psychologists have since been able to study how a skilled examiner can "affect an attitudinal shift" (i.e., brainwash) to a "subject of diminished capacity" (i.e., a tired and confused kid). A variety of exchanges between Peter and the examiners went something like this:

Peter: I couldn't have done anything like that last night. I just couldn't. Maybe your machine is wrong.

Police: No, Peter. The machine's not wrong because it's just a recording of your mind. You understand? These charts just tell us what's going on inside you.

Peter: Well I don't understand it. I'm sure I couldn't have done it. I don't remember it. If I had done it, I'd tell you. I'm not purposely trying to deny anything. I just don't remember . . . I don't know.

Later, as the interrogation got more aggressive, the ordeal began to take more of a toll on Peter. The following types of exchanges occurred:

Police: Look, Peter, we just want to get at the truth. We just want you to tell us what you did last night. Did you hit her? Did you kick her?

Peter: I don't know. I could have. You say I kicked her, and I can see myself doing it . . . imagining it.

Police: No, Peter, you're not imagining anything. It's the truth, and it's just trying to work its way out. You know, we know that this is hard for you, but you gotta try. You've gotta let the truth come out. Don't fight it.

Peter: Well, maybe. Maybe I'm just having a hard time accepting it myself. I'm just not sure . . .

Later on in the interrogation, Peter finally broke down and told the police, "Well, it really looks like I did it." Naturally, while all this was going on, the real murderer was covering his tracks and trying to put as much distance between himself and the Reilys' Connecticut home as he could. Two years passed before Peter's confession was finally proven false, and the police were left with a bizarre crime, no suspects, and red faces for having relied so heavily on their coerced polygraph "evidence."

The police don't always wait for murder cases to roll around to use their magical machine, but an unsolved death can often start the gears turning in a polygrapher's head. A Georgia murder, for example, had the police stumped. There were few clues and even fewer suspects. As public pressure mounted, the police arrested a young black kid and proceeded to harass and intimidate him. They eventually strapped him to a polygraph machine and told him that the machine could tell if he was lying or telling the truth, and that if he was lying, that the machine would electrocute him!

Now you and I may laugh at such an obvious trick, but remember that this was a poor, uneducated kid who had never been more than ten miles away from his home in rural south Georgia. Quite simply, he panicked. He really thought that the polygraph machine would electrocute him, so he admitted to everything that the police asked him about. And what was the result of this sham? Suffice it to say that prosecutors, judges, and juries don't put much faith in blatantly coerced confessions. The kid was released, and the police were back to square one.

Then there is the case of the police in Radnor, Pennsylvania, who wanted to get a quick confession out of a suspect they had just apprehended. Instead of using a real polygraph machine, however, they decided to make one of their own. One cop got a metal colander (like you would use to drain spaghetti) and attached a couple of pieces of wire to it. They ran these wires to the back of a Xerox machine and taped them in place. Finally, they typed "HE'S LYING" on a piece of paper and placed it in the machine so that it could be copied repeatedly. With their "polygraph machine" ready to go, police sat the suspect down, put the colander on his head, and began their interrogation. Whenever they received an answer they didn't care for, one of the cops would hit the "copy" button, and out would pop the message "HE'S LYING." Convinced that the machine could read his mind, the suspect confessed.

A variation of this trick has been used by police officers in several states. When they believe they have apprehended a naive suspect, the officers will wrap the squad car's microphone cable around the suspect's arm and begin the "interrogation." Unwanted answers are easily contradicted by one of the officers surreptitiously pressing the TRANSMIT button on the microphone. Pressing this button activates a red light on the car's radio, and the officer will say, "See there? See that red light? That says you're lying. You're not lying to me are you? Let's try it again." This little scenario will continue either until the suspect confesses or the officer thinks he's not getting anywhere.

SOME ALARMING STATISTICS

So you see, you don't even need a real polygraph machine to force a confession out of a suspect. These case studies should have convinced you that polygraph exams and examiners are fallible, and that you should approach these exams with a great deal of caution. But if none of this has convinced you yet, perhaps this sobering statistic will: it has been estimated that 40 to 50 percent of truthful individuals have been misdiagnosed by examiners. In other words, if you are a suspect in a criminal investigation, you have a one-in-two chance of being labeled "deceptive," even if you have no knowledge whatsoever of the crime. What's more, the Office of Technology Assessment (OTA), an arm of the federal government that analyzes and evaluates current technology, reviewed more than four thousand bibliographic entries concerning polygraph exams and found that only thirty-five to forty met any of the basic scientific criteria for a properly controlled research experiment. And of these forty or so articles, OTA found that the polygraph's ability to detect lies was as low as 50.6 percent (I can *guess* and be right 50 percent of the time!), and its ability to detect the truth ranged from a high of 94.1 percent to a dismal low of 12.5 percent.

These figures should shock you because thousands of these exams are given in the United States every working day. The polygraph industry rakes in millions of dollars every year—largely at the expense of decent, law-abiding citizens. Of course, if the polygraph machine really worked, there wouldn't be any need for me to write this book or for you to read it.

Polygraphers will tell you that their machine is correct 90 to 95 percent of the time, but let's look at what that really means. Imagine a situation in which 1,000 suspects are rounded up, but only 50 of them are actually guilty of a crime (which they all deny). If we assume that the polygraph validity rate is 90 percent for both guilty and innocent individuals, then 45 members of the guilty group will be correctly identified, and five will beat the test. Of the 950 innocent suspects, however, 95 will be misidentified as guilty! Remember, too, that these figures all assume that polygraphers are right 90 percent of the time. Imagine how many more innocent people are misclassified as a polygrapher's "correct" rate drops to 80, 70, or even 50 percent!

No matter what they tell you, polygraph examiners cannot be correct 100 percent of the time. They cannot always be correct because they are human, and humans make mistakes. But should the innocent suffer because the polygrapher didn't get a good night's sleep or because his child is at home in bed with the flu? For that matter, should an innocent individual be misidentified because he (or she) had a bad night's sleep or has a sick child?

BEATING THE BOX

Is there anything we can do to protect ourselves? You bet there is! Thousands of people have learned how to beat the box, and so can you. It's really not very hard; it just takes a little concentration and practice.

A man by the name of Floyd Fay, who was wrongly convicted of murder based on a polygraph exam spent two years behind bars before he was cleared. In that time, he became an expert in beating polygraph exams. In fact, he got so good at it that he taught other inmates his techniques. (Inmates are given polygraph exams often concerning violations of prison rules. Knowing how to beat a test can mean the difference between staying at one facility and being transferred to a maximum-security prison with the really hard-core offenders.) By his account, Fay coached twenty-seven inmates scheduled to take polygraph exams; all freely admitted to him that they were indeed guilty of the charges (which were usually drug related). After about twenty minutes of instruction, twenty-three of the twenty-seven managed to beat the test, which equates to a very respectable 85 percent success rate!

The rest of this book is dedicated to the practical aspects of the polygraph: what it is, how it works, and how you can beat it. Even if you remember only a little bit of the information herein, you will still be better prepared should you ever find yourself the unfortunate target of a criminal investigation, and you will have much less reason to fear a "preemployment screening" or an "aperiodic honesty check." If you read carefully, practice, and keep your wits about you, then in no time at all, you should have the skills necessary to beat the box!

CHAPTER THREE

THE INSTRUMENT AND THE EXAMINER

"On a more pragmatic level, the lie detector does work as long as the subject believes it works. A good examiner scares the crap out of you. It's theater."

—Leonard Saxe, principal author of the OTA's 1983 polygraph validity study

Up to this point, I have told you to be both cautious and skeptical of the polygraph machine. In all fairness, however, you don't really have to be afraid of the machine—only the operator. You see, the machine itself is a very reliable instrument that can accurately measure and record your respiration, perspiration, pulse, and skin conductance (for five thousand dollars, it ought to be able to do something well). In fact, no one I know of has ever criticized the actual machine unless the pen plotter ran out of ink or the chart-drive jammed.

Criticisms abound, however, when one person uses these innocuous physiological tracings to infer that another person is lying. In other words, the fault lies solely with the polygraph examiner, not the polygraph machine. This is important to remember if you are taking a polygraph exam and a polygrapher says, "No, the machine doesn't make mistakes. It can't lie." You should quickly remind yourself that it's not the machine you are worried about—it's the examiner. Let's take a look at the machine and its operator.

THE POLYGRAPH MACHINE: WHAT IT IS AND HOW IT WORKS

People are often impressed with or intimidated by the polygraph machine when they first see it because it is such a complicated-looking piece of electronic hardware. By comparison, my VCR is also a pretty complicated-looking piece of electronic hardware, but I don't know anyone who is overly impressed with it or threatened by it.

Is this a fair comparison? Probably not, because people see VCRs every day in their homes, in magazine advertisements, in department stores, and in television commercials. Most people, however, will see a polygraph machine only once—on a small table next to a hard chair in a sparsely furnished room. Remember, too, that VCRs and polygraph machines will most likely be encountered under vastly different circumstances. Most people would not be afraid to go to a shopping mall if they knew VCRs were sold there. Most people are very anxious, however, if they know that they have to go to a downtown office building or hotel room to take part in a polygraph examination. In other words, going to a shopping mall is not normally an anxiety-arousing experience; going to a polygraph exam is.

But you no longer have to be afraid of the machine! They are not much more complicated than a VCR, and there is not any great amount of variation from model to model.

Most polygraph machines in use today are portable and are about the size and shape of a standard briefcase.

On one side of the machine is an approximately eight-inch-wide (this varies with respect to the manufacturer) ribbon of paper on which your responses are recorded. When the test begins, this paper will travel across the top of the machine (under a series of pens) and exit through a side opening. This gives the examiner easy access to your plotted responses during the exam, and it gives him a hard copy of your responses for future examination or reference. This component of the machine is called the *chart drive.*

Suspended above the chart are anywhere from three to five or more pens that fluctuate with respect to your level of arousal. This is called the *pen plotter,* and it may differ from machine to machine, depending on how many *channels* are being recorded. A three-channel machine, for example, will usually record heart rate, skin conductance, and rate of breathing. A four-channel machine does the same thing, but it may take two separate recordings of respiration. This is done through *pneumographs* that are strapped around the body. A pneumograph is nothing more than a rubber tube that expands and contracts as you breathe. These tubes are placed around the chest (three-channel machine) or around the chest and abdomen (four-channel machine) in order to accurately gauge any irregularities in your breathing patterns. Cardiovascular activity (heart rate or blood pressure or both) is recorded with a *sphygmomanometer* (blood pressure cuff) placed around the biceps. Skin conductance is measured by placing *electrodes* on the fingertips. These are generally held in place with Velcro, and the examiner may or may not apply some sort of conducting jelly to the fingertips before they are attached.

The pneumographs, blood pressure cuff, and electrodes are all wired to the machine so that your responses can be fed to the pen plotter. Most machines will electronically enhance one or more of these leads before they reach the pen plotter. The blood pressure reading is enhanced, for example, so that the cuff does not have to be fully inflated, which would restrict blood flow to your lower arm and hand. Skin conductance may also be enhanced so that the peaks and valleys recorded on the chart are more pronounced and easier to read. Some have said that this enhancement alters the pen plotter's tracings and, therefore, should not be used. This is really an unfair charge because the electronic enhancement is not altering the patterns or tracings, it is merely amplifying them. Think of it this way: if you can't hear the quieter sections of a cassette tape you are playing, you just turn up the volume. You haven't altered the music, you have just made it easier to hear. The polygraph machine works the same way. It "turns up the volume" on your physiological reactions so they are easier to read and interpret.

Consider, though, that if you turn up the volume on a bad cassette, you still have a bad cassette, only louder. Likewise, you can enhance a person's physiological measurements all you want, but it won't make you any more accurate in formulating an assessment of that person's veracity. No amount of electronic gadgetry will have an appreciable effect on polygraph validity because the polygraph exam itself is an inherently bad system based on a variety of bad techniques.

THE POLYGRAPH EXAMINER: WHO HE IS AND HOW HE WORKS

Does a career involving a minimum amount of education beyond a high school diploma (six weeks of training and a nine-month apprenticeship) that can lead to a fifty- to sixty-thousand-dollar-a year career sound too good to be true? Well, it's not. All you have to do is run down to your nearest polygraph training school and sign up for "a challenging and rewarding career in the fast-paced world of lie detection!"

Despite what you might think, not all polygraphers are former police officers, military men, private detectives, or CIA agents. Many are just your average high school graduates, college dropouts, or college graduates who realized they could make a lot more money as polygraph examiners than as assistant managers at the local fast-food joint.

In one respect, these types of examiners may treat their examinees more fairly, because they don't have the preconceived notions that seem to be inherent in a lot of former cops, for instance. One examiner who had been a police officer was captured on a hidden camera saying that he could usually tell within five minutes of meeting a suspect whether or not that suspect was guilty. This is the ultimate in polygrapher arrogance. If the examiner can really make that distinction almost immediately after meeting someone, why does he need the machine? I suspect that police officers are more prone to make this type of error than "civilians," because they have encountered the criminal element on an almost daily basis.

This is not to say that civilian polygraphers do not make determinations of guilt before the test has even been run—they do. In fact, I don't know of anyone who can meet an individual for the first time and not form some sort of opinion about that person. It's human nature. This is precisely why no polygrapher can be completely objective as he scores and interprets the charts. His personal biases and opinions are incorporated automatically (consciously or unconsciously) into his decisions, whether or not he recognizes it. He may say his decisions are totally objective, but how do we know he doesn't harbor some personal dislike toward men with long hair, Mexican-Americans, divorced women, Catholics, or any of a hundred other demographic characteristics? The fact is, we don't know, and we can't tell unless we ask him, point blank, whether or not he is biased against a particular group of people. And even if he tells us he's not, how do we know he's not lying? Maybe we could strap a polygraph machine on him and give him a taste of his own medicine . . .

Civilian Training

It is difficult to talk about civilian polygraph training because there are so many theories and techniques taught at so many independent schools. But one major disagreement exists between the competing Reid and Backster organizations.

The Reid school trains its students to use what is known as global scoring. This entails: A) reading the suspect's case file and other supplemental materials, B) conducting the pretest interview, C) formulating the test questions, D) administering the test, E) conducting the post-test interview, F) considering all the behavioral patterns exhibited by the suspect during steps B through E, G) evaluating the polygraph charts, and H) reaching a final determination of deceptiveness or nondeceptiveness. The Reid school also teaches that special attention should be given to the behavioral patterns emitted by the suspect because it is the examiner who actually detects lies. The machine may provide the charts, but it is the examiner's training, insightfulness, and experience that create an overall impression.

The Backster school, on the other hand, deemphasizes global scoring in favor of straight chart interpretations. Teachers at the Backster school will not have students memorize long lists of "deceptive" behaviors, nor will they tell them to give their subjective impressions more weight than the actual charts. At a Backster school, students will learn how to score a chart numerically and base decisions entirely on the data provided by the charts.

If I were ever suspected of a crime and chose to submit to a polygraph exam, I would much rather have a Backster-trained examiner administer it for two reasons: 1) I would know that he was using the most objective methods available to score my charts, and 2) I would not have to worry about whether or not I arrived late for the session, how I was dressed, or whether I sat with my legs crossed or not. Reid examiners will take all of these factors into consideration; properly trained Backster examiners will not.

Of course, another problem is that not all polygraph examiners are taught at either of those schools. At least with Reid- and Backster-trained examiners, you have some idea what they are looking for and how your exam will be scored. The hundreds of other independent schools (which, by the way, usually need no state licensing) and police forces may teach totally different techniques. I can easily envision a school that uses some of Reid's ideas, some of Backster's ideas, and some ideas that a staff member happened to pick up in an introductory psychology course taught at the local community college. Some schools might emphasize the GSR channel, others might emphasize changes in blood pressure.

This lack of standardization can only hurt the polygraph industry in the long run as more and more unaccredited schools turn out more and more unqualified examiners. Furthermore, there is no real "continuing education" in the polygraph industry. The implied message is that once you have graduated, you know all you need to know for the rest of your life.

There are journals that publish pro polygraph articles almost exclusively (*Journal of Polygraph Studies, Polygraph, Journal of Polygraph Science*), but most of those articles should be taken with a grain of salt. The *Journal of Polygraph Science*, for example, recently ran a piece entitled, "Clothes Make the Polygraphist."

What is the overall evaluation of civilian polygraph training? Like many things in life, some is good, some is bad, and some is so substandard that it is a real dilemma for the truly committed professionals who are trying to raise the polygraph industry above the realm of technological mysticism. The most important step the civilian polygraph industry can take is to adopt some sort of standardization for tests so that all polygraphers adhere to at least some basic methodology. As it stands now, polygraph results are a lot like psychiatric opinions of insanity: there will never be a consensus. If you've been judged deceptive three times, keep looking and you'll almost certainly be able to find three examiners who will vouch for your truthfulness.

Military Training

Unlike civilian polygraph training, the military has only one school that teaches FBI, Secret Service, National Security Agency, and military investigators. This polygraph brain trust is located in Building 3165 at Fort McClellan, Alabama, home of the U.S. Army Military Police School (USAMPS). The polygraph is taken very seriously there, a fact fresh recruits learn quickly. Anyone uttering taboo words such as "Ouija Board," "hot question," "squiggly lines," "innocent," "guilty," "thingamabob," or "lie detector" is forced to make a contribution to the class fund. Upon graduation, the accumulated money goes toward a graduation picnic.

Not surprisingly, the training at Fort McClellan's polygraph school is militaristic and rigorously structured. Instead of the typical six-week course administered by civilian schools, Fort McClellan trains for fourteen weeks. Weeks one through four include lectures on law, semantics, ethics, physiology, psychology, pharmacology, testing procedures, and machine operation and maintenance. Weeks five through fourteen are devoted to practice sessions so that the student can apply what he is supposed to have learned.

The results of this strict training are evident: Fort McClellan is widely acclaimed as the best polygraph training facility in the world. In fact, the world often comes to Fort McClellan in the form of foreign government agents: Taiwan, Israel, Venezuela, and South Korea have all sent agents to the infamous Building 3165 for training. There is no doubt that polygraph examiners trained at Fort McClellan are better prepared than the majority of civilian examiners.

Should you be concerned, then, if you ever find yourself across the table from a McClellan graduate? I don't think so. As long as you can control your emotions and remain calm, you should never have to fear any polygraph examiner—no matter how qualified he is. Remember, Fort McClellan may turn out the best polygraphers in the world, but the underlying theory of what they teach is still flawed. No amount of training can compensate for the fact that there are no reliable physiological responses correlated with telling a lie. Of course, polygraph examiners will never admit to this. They will instead try to overtly or covertly coerce you into believing you are helpless against their advanced technology and knowledge.

Don't believe a word of it! If they were as good as they say they are, then we would have no more need for judges or juries or any other part of the judicial system. A polygrapher could just test suspect after suspect until he found a guilty one, and then throw him in jail. This hasn't happened yet, nor is it likely to—especially since the machine is so easy to beat in the first place.

THE TESTS

If you should ever do some additional reading in the field of polygraphy, you will come across a number of phrases that are synonyms for "polygraph test." Among these are "polygraph exam," "polygraph screening," "polygraph evaluation," "polygraph interrogation," and, occasionally, "deceptograph." While these are all useful synonyms, it should be noted that most of them are technically inadequate.

WHEN IS A TEST NOT A TEST?

The American Psychological Association (APA) is very exacting when it comes to terminology. Do you see a significant difference between the words "test," "screening," and "interrogation"? The APA certainly does. Only the phrase "psychological test" has a clear-cut, standardized definition.

To be properly labeled a psychological test, an examination must meet four basic criteria: standardized method of administration, immediate recording of behavior, objective scoring, and external validity. Using these criteria, can we properly call a polygraph exam a psychological test? Let's find out.

Standardized method of administration. The number of training schools and varying techniques violates this rule.

Immediate recording of behavior. The polygraph does immediately record the rate of perspiration, respiration, and heartbeat, but if the examiner is using a global scoring technique, then "overt psychomotor behaviors" may not be recorded for minutes or even hours after the formal examination has concluded.

Objective scoring. Only a small subset of today's polygraph exams are scored objectively. The vast majority of determinations are made by combining chart data with the examiner's subjective impressions of the subject's personality.

External validity. There are no data demonstrating the validity of an examiner's subjective appraisal of veracity.

Judging from these criteria, it appears that a polygraph "test" is really not a test at all. But if it's not a test, then what should we call it? Perhaps the word that best describes the whole polygraph procedure is "interrogation." The accused is not being tested per se; he/she is merely taking part in a data-gathering session. The polygrapher's job is to pick out the relevant from the irrelevant. Unfortunately, whenever a polygrapher compares and combines objective polygraph data with subjective clinical assumptions, all of the criteria for a valid psychological test are violated. Consequently, polygraph tests, for the most part, are best described as interrogations. Realize that when I refer to them as "polygraph tests," it is merely for the sake of brevity.

TYPES OF POLYGRAPH TEST QUESTIONS

Almost all polygraph exams are composed of three types of questions: relevant, irrelevant, and control. The primary difference has to do with the frequency and placement of each of these types of questions. Some examiners, however, will administer an exam that contains only one type of question, the guilty knowledge question, which is used to determine whether you know certain facts about a crime that you couldn't possibly know unless you were the guilty party. As we examine all four of these types of questions, pay careful attention to the characteristics of each; you will need to be able to identify the type of question being asked in order to defeat a polygraph exam. At the end of this section are some sample tests, which I encourage you to run through a number of times in order to get the feel of how a polygraph exam works and to test your knowledge. Remember, polygraph examiners rely on the assumption that they know more about how an exam works than you do. Don't allow them this advantage over you. Knowledge is power! The more you know about polygraph examinations, the better off you will be.

Relevant Questions

Relevant questions are those which are directly related to the focus of an investigation. As such, a relevant question can be very narrow and specific ("Did you steal the three hundred dollars from the cash register on the evening of July 23?") or, when the area of interest may be an individual's entire background, very broad ("Have you ever been disciplined on the job for alcohol or drug abuse?"). Relevant questions are usually easy to spot because they will almost always relate to whatever incident (or crime) is under investigation. One exception to this rule involves interrogations conducted by intelligence agencies. Should you ever find yourself under examination by an intelligence agent, you should prepare yourself for questions concerning unauthorized contact with foreign intelligence agents or involvement in Communist activities. Questions in an intelligence screening might also deal with aspects of an individual's life that would make him/her susceptible to blackmail. It is important to note, however, that when several relevant questions must cover a variety of equally important issues (e.g., political leanings, criminal record, and so on), the individual under examination is not expected to exhibit elevated physiological responses to all of them; and the relevant questions that do not evoke higher-than-normal responses are used later as control questions.

This brings up an important point about the relationship between relevant, irrelevant, and control questions. They can switch from one category to another depending on the specific context in which they are used. Consequently, any questions presented here as an example of a particular category may change categories under different circumstances or even at different times during the same interview.

Suppose the retail store where you work has been experiencing a lot of lost (and presumably stolen) inventory. You have voluntarily submitted to a polygraph exam, and you are asked the following question: "Have you ever consumed alcoholic beverages during working hours?" Is this a relevant question? In this instance, it is not. It is a control question designed to make you feel anxious about the consequences of being caught drinking on the job. And since many employees will have the occasional beer at lunch or glass of wine at an office party, it does work well to raise doubts in your mind and make you unusually anxious.

Now consider a different situation. You are a delivery driver for an antiques store. One Friday afternoon, you crash the truck into a tree and leave the scene of the accident. Later that evening, you phone your employer and tell him you "blacked out" while driving and don't really know what happened. Suspicious, your employer asks you to take a polygraph exam in order to prove your innocence. You agree, and the examiner asks you the following: "Have you ever consumed alcoholic beverages during working hours?" In this instance, this is a relevant question, because drinking could very well be a cause of the accident and is therefore relevant to the issue under investigation.

Irrelevant Questions

Irrelevant questions, while seemingly innocuous, serve a very important purpose in that they allow an examiner to chart an individual's normal, baseline level of arousal. A comparison can then be made between baseline arousal and arousal brought about by the relevant questions. In order to maximize the difference between response levels, irrelevant questions are designed to have very little emotional impact on an individual. A typical irrelevant questions would be, "Is today Friday?" or "Are we in the state of Florida?" Of course, irrelevant questions may become relevant, depending on an individual's response. So, for example, if you show unusually strong emotion to the question, "Is your name John Smith," the examiner may suspect that you are hiding behind a false identity and decide to treat that question as a relevant one instead.

Control Questions

Like irrelevant questions, control questions are used for comparison with relevant questions. The critical difference is that control questions are not used to establish a baseline, but to elicit a strong emotional response. In order to effectively defeat a polygraph exam, you must be able to recognize any control questions that may come your way. One type concerns what is considered to be related indirectly to the issue under investigation. For example, in a criminal investigation involving the theft of money from a desk drawer, a control question might be, "Have you ever stolen anything of value in your life?" For an insider trading probe, a control question might be, "Have you ever betrayed a confidence?" Again, control questions and relevant questions are easily interchangeable, depending on the circumstances. This has led to controversy among polygraphers over the use of so-called "inclusive" versus "exclusive" controls. Inclusive controls probe the incident under investigation indirectly. For example, an incident involving the theft of three hundred dollars from a cash register could produce the following:

Q. Have you ever stolen money from an employer? (Inclusive control.)

Q. Did you remove the three hundred dollars from the cash register? (Relevant.)

Exclusive controls, on the other hand, cover a period of time exclusive of the incident under investigation. So continuing with the cash register example, we get:

Q. Before the age of eighteen, did you ever take anything of value? (Exclusive control.)

The controversy surrounding inclusive versus exclusive controls involves the concept of "psychological separation." Some polygraphers argue that suspects under investigation treat inclusive controls like relevant questions (i.e., they do not treat them as separate, independent categories). This "lumping together" of the controls with the relevants would defeat the purpose of the control question and thus invalidate the test. This is the position taken by the federal government, so you should never encounter inclusive control questions during a government interrogation. Private polygraph firms, however, will often use both inclusive and exclusive controls.

Concealed Information Questions

The use of concealed information questions is based on the assumption that the guilty individual will know (and remember) specific details of a crime that no innocent person could possibly know. Such information might include details about the site of the crime or the means of committing it, such as the technique used to enter a locked building. An apartment burglary, for example, might generate the following concealed information question: "A piece of jewelry was taken during the crime. If you are the guilty person, you know what that jewelry was. Was it A) a silver earring, B) a pearl necklace, C) a diamond ring, D) a gold bracelet, or E) a gold cross and chain?" It is hypothesized that a guilty individual will respond differently to the correct (relevant) alternative. Innocent suspects, due to their lack of specific knowledge about the crime, should respond fairly equally to each of the five alternatives.

TYPES OF TESTS

The four types of questions outlined above form the basis of the three different polygraph testing techniques: the Relevant/Irrelevant Technique (R/I), the Control Question Technique (CQT), and the Guilty Knowledge Technique (GKT).

Each has its strengths and weaknesses, and each works best under specific conditions. Therefore, you should anticipate which technique you will most likely encounter in order to be adequately prepared on the day of the test.

The Relevant/Irrelevant (R/I) Technique

The R/I Technique was once the most frequently used form of lie detection in the United States. It was commonly exploited by personnel directors for pre-employment screening interviews, and had what was probably the broadest potential of the three techniques. That has changed.

In 1988, Congress passed a law (HR1212) called the "Polygraph Protection Act." Among other things, it made it illegal to use polygraph examinations for preemployment screening unless the employer is hiring for potentially dangerous or security-sensitive work. Pharmaceutical companies, for example, are excluded, as are security-type companies that are hiring night watchmen, armored car drivers, etc.

So far, HR1212 has driven a number of polygraph companies out of business, and it has forced budget cutbacks and wholesale employee terminations in those that wish to survive. There is still a possibility, however, that you will have to undergo an R/I test, especially if you want to work for the government.

As the name implies, the R/I Technique uses only two types of questions: relevant and irrelevant. According to R/I theory, deceptive individuals will show greater reactions to the relevant questions, while nondeceptive individuals, having nothing to fear, will show similar patterns of reactions to all the questions. To say that this technique is flawed is an understatement. First of all, most people have no trouble differentiating between relevant and irrelevant questions, so both innocent and guilty individuals have a high probability of responding differently to the relevant questions. If the guilty and innocent alike respond strongly to relevant questions, what is driving this response? Perhaps it is surprise over the question or anger that the question is being asked. A variety of emotions could account for an elevated response.

Despite these flaws, the R/I test has its proponents, and it is still commonly used. In screening examinations, relevant questions will generally pertain to past job behaviors as well as current job qualifications. The following are some of the relevant questions usually used in preemployment screening tests. (Be sure to note how many of these could be control questions in a different situation.)

Q. Did you falsify any information on your application?

Q. In the last five years, did you ever steal any money or merchandise from a previous employer?

Q. Have you ever been fired from a job?

Q. Are you seeking a job with this company for any reason other than legitimate employment?

Q. Since the age of eighteen, have you ever been convicted of a crime?

Q. Have you used marijuana in the last ___ years?

Q. Have you used any other narcotic illegally in the past ___ years?

Q. Are you seeking a permanent position with this company?

Q. Have you deliberately lied in answering any of these questions?

The R/I Technique is used by employers as an aperiodic honesty check as well. Although most employers use honesty checks to determine the extent of employee theft or on-the-job drug use, others like to assess such things as employee satisfaction and commitment. Aperiodic honesty checks are composed almost entirely of relevant questions; apparent deception to any of the items is usually explored further. Some questions that have been used in aperiodic honesty checks are:

Q. Are you satisfied with your present job and working conditions?

Q. Do you consider yourself to be a loyal company employee?

Q. Are you aware of any specific employee dissension?

Q. Have you ever witnessed a fellow employee deliberately damaging company property?

Q. Do you have any unauthorized keys?

Q. Do you intend to stay with this employer?

Q. Have you ever stolen merchandise from this company?

Q. Do you know any employee who has been revealing company secrets to a competitor?

Q. Have you ever put merchandise in the trash for later pickup?

Q. Do you suspect another employee of stealing from this company?

The Control Question Technique (CQT)

As polygraph theory evolved and the problems with the R/I Technique began to surface, a new test was developed. Both the relevant and irrelevant questions were retained, but a control question was added to the mix. As discussed above, control questions are designed to cause arousal in both nondeceptive and deceptive individuals. They usually probe for past misdeeds of the same general nature as the crime being investigated. Because it is assumed that we have all committed a few minor transgressions throughout our lives, truly innocent suspects are supposed to be more doubtful or concerned about the control questions than the relevant questions. This concern is thought to be reflected in higher peaks on the polygraph chart around the control question areas. Guilty suspects, on the other hand, should show higher peaks around the relevant question areas—a reflection of their concern toward the relevant details of the crime. Many control questions cover a long period of time ("Before the age of eighteen, did you ever commit a serious crime?"), which is intended to make the suspect even more doubtful about the truthfulness of his answers. After all, who can remember every possible misdeed he might have committed over eighteen years?

Believe it or not, you yourself play a part in making the control questions so anxiety-arousing. During the informal interview that precedes nearly every polygraph exam, the examiner will develop and review all the test questions with you so that "there will be no misunderstandings during the actual test." Actually, you are being carefully manipulated to either A) be deceptive in answering the control questions, or B) be so concerned about your recollections that you become overly anxious.

Here's how it works: the examiner will pose a very broad question during the pretest interview, such as, "Have you ever stolen anything in your life?" Most people will sift through a lifetime of recollections in search of an instance where they might have stolen something. Now, consider the two ways you can answer this question. If you say "yes," you run the risk of letting the examiner know you have stolen in the past, which could easily prejudice his opinion of you. On the other hand, if you answer "no," you will worry that the examiner doesn't believe you and will assume that you are hiding something. Consequently, most people will admit to "small crimes"—taking pens home from work, stealing pocket change as a child, etc. This is exactly what the examiner wants you to do. He will dismiss these small crimes as being inconsequential and rephrase the original question: "Other than what we have discussed, have you ever stolen anything in your life?" Now the anxiety can set in. Straight arrows who really haven't stolen anything will worry that they may have overlooked something; those who have committed real crimes (but didn't admit to them) will worry because they are forced to lie.

Either way, the polygrapher wins. He has gotten you to provide an elevated response to the control question, which he can then compare with the relevant questions. You fell into his trap. The polygrapher, of course, will not tell you that this manipulation is taking place. He will stress that each question must be answered completely with a simple yes or no response and that the machine will record any doubts or misgivings. He will try to persuade you that he only wants you to tell the truth. In reality, though, the examiner is counting on you to be moderately doubtful or intentionally deceptive. This is accomplished by making the control questions vague and difficult to answer with an unqualified "no."

It is debatable whether the addition of control questions makes a polygraph test any more valid. The polygraph industry thinks so, but one man who doesn't is University of Minnesota psychologist David T. Lykken. He argues that anyone formulating questions for a CQT must make three important assumptions about the examinee (Lykken, *Nature*, 1984, p. 684): 1) The subject will answer deceptively several questions referring to his or her past. Lykken argues that some people really have led lives of utmost integrity, so these control questions could not serve their intended purpose. 2) A subject who can answer the relevant questions truthfully will be more disturbed by the controls than the relevant questions. Lykken argues that it is unreasonable to predict with any confidence which questions a person will find more disturbing. 3) Guilty persons, who must answer relevant questions deceptively, will show stronger reactions to the relevant questions than the controls. Lykken again argues that we really don't know which questions a person will find more disturbing.

The Guilty Knowledge Technique (GKT)

This test is the least likely to be encountered. Lykken first proposed this technique in 1959, but it has never really been accepted by the polygraph industry. The fundamental difference between the GKT and other techniques is that a GKT interrogation attempts to detect the presence of guilty knowledge—not lying. For example, in the burglarized apartment scenario mentioned earlier, an innocent person should respond fairly equally to each of the five alternatives (silver earring, pearl necklace, diamond ring, gold bracelet, or gold cross and chain) and would have only one chance in five of reacting most strongly to the correct alternative (i.e., actual item of jewelry stolen). With ten multiple choice items of this type, an innocent person would have less than one chance in ten million of reacting most strongly to all ten correct alternatives if he or she did not possess guilty knowledge.

Some people want the GKT to take the place of the CQT. One advantage is that it may reduce the number of false positives—innocent persons labeled guilty—because it would be almost statistically impossible for an innocent person to coincidentally react to the correct alternative enough times to achieve a "guilty" determination from an examiner. Unfortunately, say the GKT's critics, this is a double-edged sword because the GKT also fails to detect a large number of guilty suspects. Critics also complain that the GKT may not be widely applicable. It obviously could not be used as a preemployment screening test.

Other oft-mentioned problems with the GKT are the concept of "guilty" knowledge and the difficulty in making the test valid. Concerning the former, critics charge that knowledge about an incident may not differentiate between a guilty and an innocent person where, for example, a suspect is present at the scene of a crime but claims someone else did it. Also, the test becomes useless when the press covers a sensational crime in such a way that all the relevant details become public knowledge. When addressing the latter issue, many police investigators/polygraphers claim that it is just too difficult to come up with enough good questions about a crime to clearly implicate a suspect. Furthermore, they say, if enough information is obtained to create a six- or ten-item GKT test, there is still no guarantee that the suspect will not claim to have had these facts revealed to him in other parts of the investigation—or that the suspect will even remember such details in the first place.

All things considered, you probably do not have to worry about being subjected to a GKT exam. The polygraph industry doesn't like it, so it is rarely used. Instructions for beating a GKT will still be presented in the countermeasures section, just in case you face that occasional polygrapher who favors the procedure.

PRACTICE TESTS

The following pages contain practice tests for R/I, CQT, and GKT polygraph exams. Each begins with a short scenario, which you should read and imagine to be actually occurring in your life. For the R/I test, try to determine whether each question is relevant (R) or irrelevant (I). For the CQT test, try to label each question as relevant (R), irrelevant (I), or control (C). Answers are provided at the end of the chapter. Later, after you have read the section on countermeasures, you can come back to these tests and practice your skills.

Although it is not necessary, you may find it useful to practice with a friend. Try to mimic a real-life polygraph setting as much as possible. The more you practice, the better prepared you will be. All the GKT test questions are relevant, so there is not much to be gained by going over these tests until you have read the section on countermeasures. A word of warning: GKT tests favor innocent suspects, so, if you are innocent, the best countermeasure is to be yourself. If you are guilty, then you should know that the GKT can be very hard to beat, especially if you have a good memory for detail and remember exactly how the crime was committed. Practice of your countermeasures is essential.

R/I Scenario

You have applied for an entry-level position of Quality Control Analyst at ABC Pharmaceuticals, a midwestern pharmaceutical wholesaler. Although your work history and résumé are well above average, the personnel director has asked you to submit to a polygraph examination because your job will put you in constant contact with a variety of drugs. Because this is a preemployment screening examination, there is no pretest interview. The examiner has you wired up and is ready to begin.

Questions	R or I
1. Is today Tuesday?	_____
2. Are you sitting in a chair?	_____
3. Have you ever stolen merchandise from a place where you've worked?	_____
4. Have you ever consumed alcoholic beverages while on the job?	_____
5. Is your mother's name Sarah?	_____
6. Do you live in an apartment?	_____
7. Have you ever been convicted of a crime?	_____
8. Was it raining this morning?	_____
9. Have you ever smoked marijuana on the job?	_____

10. Are you wearing glasses? _____
11. Do you consider yourself trustworthy? _____
12. Do you have red hair? _____
13. Have you ever been through an alcohol or drug treatment program? _____
14. Do you watch television? _____
15. Thus far, have you deliberately lied to any of the questions I have asked you? _____

CQT Scenario 1

You work on the dock unloading trucks for A.A. Blair's, a chain of five discount department stores. Business couldn't be better. Christmas sales were far above projections, and everyone's morale is high. Unfortunately, there has been some whispering around the water cooler that a lot of merchandise cannot be accounted for.

The year-end inventory confirms the bad news—there is more than ten thousand dollars worth of merchandise on the books that is not in the warehouse. Some have suggested that a driver is working with one of the dock workers to defraud the company.

The store manager conducted interviews with all the dock personnel, but no one was talking. Reluctantly, the manager brought in a polygrapher to handle the problem. Everyone so far has passed, and you are about to begin your test.

Questions   **R, I, or C**
1. Are you one hundred years old? _____
2. Is your name Scott? _____
3. Have you ever "covered" for a fellow employee by falsifying his/her time card? _____
4. Have you ever falsified inventory records for personal gain? _____
5. Were you born in Baltimore? _____

6. Have you ever stolen merchandise
   from this company?   _____
7. Do you drink coffee?   _____
8. Do you know of anyone who is trying to
   defraud this company?   _____
9. Do you have any children?   _____
10. Have you falsified your employment
    application in any manner?   _____
11. Have you ever hidden merchandise in
    the trash to be picked up later?   _____
12. Are your parents divorced?   _____
13. Have you ever called in sick when
    actually you were not?   _____
14. Do you work on a dock?   _____
15. Have you ever tried to defraud this
    store in any manner?   _____

CQT Scenario 2

After three years of hard work, you have finally been named senior administrative assistant to the chairman of the Bart County School Board. There were three other candidates competing for the position, but your knowledge of the county's computer systems pushed you over the top.

Not long after you began work at your new position, strange things started to happen. Computer files were being wiped out, programs wouldn't run correctly, and the department's specialized financial software was subjected to two different viruses.

The department heads were convinced that all this vandalism was performed by a disgruntled employee. Unfortunately, most of the department's employees have limited access to the computers—your access is unlimited and totally unsupervised. Although there is no logical reason for you to be behind this wave of vandalism, you are the first to be administered a polygraph exam by the county police.

Questions   **R, I, or C**

  1. Do you have a sister?   _____
  2. Before the age of eighteen, did you
     ever purposefully manipulate another
     person's software?   _____
  3. Have you ever used the department's
     computers for unauthorized purposes?   _____
  4. Are both your feet on the floor?   _____
  5. Do you know who is sabotaging the
     department's computer records?   _____
  6. Does one plus one equal three?   _____
  7. Are you wearing a shirt?   _____
  8. Have you ever made or received personal
     phone calls while on company time?   _____
  9. Are you happy in your present position?   _____
 10. Are your eyes brown?   _____
 11. Do you know how to drive?   _____
 12. Have you ever suspected a fellow
     employee of being under the influence
     of alcohol while on the job?   _____
 13. Do you know of people who are dissatisfied
     with their employment in the department?   _____
 14. Are you right-handed?   _____
 15. Have you ever planted a computer virus
     in the department's computer system?   _____

GKT Scenario

An apartment has been burglarized. While not admitting your guilt, you know that the apartment was #112 and that the following items were taken: cash, credit cards, a diamond ring, a Minolta camera, a pair of binoculars, a stamp collection, an electric guitar, and a tennis racket. You also know that the cash was hidden in the back of a clock and that the clock was deliberately broken. You have been arrested for the crime and are about to take a GKT polygraph exam. After the detective reads each alternative, you must repeat it and deny that it is the correct alternative (e.g., "231. No.")

Questions

1. If you are guilty of this crime, then you know the number of the apartment that was burglarized. Was it:
   a) 418
   b) 206
   c) 112
   d) 327
   e) 530

2. The cash stolen from this apartment was in a unique hiding place. If you are the guilty person, then you know where the cash was hidden. Was it:
   a) behind a picture
   b) under a trash can
   c) inside a medicine cabinet
   d) inside a clock
   e) inside an album cover

3. Something that was on the speaker close to the chair in the living room was stolen. If you are the guilty person, then you know what was stolen. Was it:
   a) a lamp
   b) a book
   c) a brass urn
   d) a pair of binoculars
   e) a jewelry box

4. A musical instrument was stolen from the apartment. If you are the guilty person, you know what that instrument was. Was it:
   a) a saxophone
   b) a guitar
   c) a harmonica
   d) a flute
   e) a violin

5. Something valuable was taken from the dining room table. If you are the guilty person, then you know what this was. Was it:

a) a television
b) an antique clock
c) a stamp collection
d) a gold pen
e) a pair of silver candlesticks

6. Some jewelry was stolen from the apartment. If you are the guilty person, you know what was stolen. Was it:

a) a silver bracelet
b) a pearl necklace
c) a pair of jade earrings
d) a gold cross and chain
e) a diamond ring

7. Something was stolen from a wallet found in the apartment. If you are the guilty person, then you know what was stolen from the wallet. Was it:

a) a driver's license
b) a key
c) money
d) credit cards
e) a traveler's check

8. Something was deliberately broken during the commission of the crime. If you are the guilty person, you know what was broken. Was it:

a) a trophy
b) a clock
c) a bottle
d) a lamp
e) a picture frame

9. A camera was stolen from the apartment. If you are the guilty person, you know what brand it was. Was it:

a) a Toshiba
b) a Nikon
c) a Canon
d) a Minolta
e) a Pentax

10. Some sporting equipment was taken from the apartment. If you are the guilty person, you know what was taken. Was it:
    a) a stopwatch
    b) a tennis racket
    c) a skateboard
    d) a bowling ball
    e) a baseball glove

Answers
R/I Scenario
    1. I
    2. I
    3. R
    4. R
    5. I
    6. I
    7. R
    8. I
    9. R
    10. I
    11. R
    12. I
    13. R
    14. I
    15. R

CQT Scenario 1
    1. I
    2. I
    3. C

4. R
5. I
6. R
7. I
8. R
9. I
10. C
11. R
12. I
13. C
14. I
15. R

CQT Scenario 2
1. I
2. C
3. R
4. I
5. R
6. I
7. I
8. C
9. R
10. I
11. I
12. C
13. C
14. I
15. R

CHAPTER FIVE

COUNTERMEASURES

> "The whole procedure requires that the subject cooperate."
>
> —R. Decker, Chief of the Federal Government's Polygraph Trainers

> "If you can control your bowels, you can control your test results."
>
> —Douglas Gene Williams, a former Oklahoma police polygrapher who now campaigns against the lie detection industry

A polygrapher's job would be so much easier if every suspect behaved like an unknowing lamb being led to slaughter. Most Americans, however, will not sit idly by while someone tries to tamper with their rights—like the right to hold down a job or the right to be treated with dignity and respect. Professional polygraph examiners hope that you never read this book—and especially this chapter—because it represents a challenge to their multimillion-dollar industry. Like a con man, the polygrapher counts on your gullibility and ignorance in order to trick you into believing his machine can magically read your thoughts.

It's time for us to stop bowing down to their Orwellian creation and fight back! It's time to make a liar of the lie detector! You took the first step in limiting a polygrapher's power over you by opening this book. The sole reason for this book's existence is to demythologize the lie detector and give you a clearer understanding of how it works—or doesn't work. I hope you spent some time going over the practice tests in the last chapter because the single most important skill you can develop to beat a lie detector test is the ability to recognize and differentiate between relevant questions, irrelevant questions, and control questions. Once you feel confident in recognizing these question categories, you can move on to countermeasures.

Countermeasures are deliberate techniques used by individuals to alter their response patterns during a polygraph examination. The list of countermeasures has grown over the years, but they all fall into three major categories: physical, cognitive, and pharmacological.

PHYSICAL COUNTERMEASURES

Because a polygrapher must infer deception from a pattern of physiological responses, any physical activity that alters a physiological response is a potential countermeasure. The trick is to know when you should enhance your responses so that you appear to be nervous (during control questions), and when you should attenuate your responses so that you appear to be calm and relaxed (during relevant questions). The following list of physical countermeasures contains a variety of popular techniques. Many have been used in university studies assessing polygraph validity.

Breathing
If you want to appear calm and truthful, you should breathe at a calm, regular pace. A polygraph chart will indicate nervousness/deception if you deviate from a slow, regular pattern in any of the following ways: inhaling deeply, breathing in shallow and erratic gasps,

momentarily holding your breath, sighing, breathing rapidly through your nose, panting with your lungs full, or gasping with your lungs empty.

Muscle Tension

To appear truthful, you should sit calmly and literally not move a muscle. You can then elevate your responses to the control questions by tensing and relaxing any of the major muscle groups (arms, thighs, abdominals, and gluteus). Note: If you are going to tense your arm as a countermeasure, do not tense the arm that has the blood pressure cuff attached. This is too easily detected. Also, you may want to try pressing your arm hard against the chair's arm (most polygraph examiners require you to sit in an armchair) because that is harder to spot than flexing your biceps. Another very effective trick is to pucker up your anus for five to ten seconds and then release. This creates a momentary elevation of blood pressure that the examiner will believe is being caused by anxiety at a particular question.

One word of caution regarding these muscle techniques: polygraph examiners have developed a counter-countermeasure to limit their effectiveness. Sometimes called a pneumatic chair or pressure chair, it consists simply of a chair with pressure sensors or strain gauges in the arms and seat. These sensors are attached to a separate pen on the polygraph that will record any unnatural muscle tension. Should you suspect that you are sitting in one of these chairs, you should alter your game plan and focus on the nonphysical countermeasures.

Pressing the Toes

Unlike tensing a major muscle group, pressing the toes against the floor usually will not be detected by a specialized chair. To appear that you are experiencing anxiety in response to a particular question, all you need to do is press your toes hard against the floor for a few seconds and then release. Polygraphers have developed a counter-countermeasure for this technique as well, and it consists of nothing more than having you place your feet on a footrest for the duration of the examination. Some examiners may even ask you to remove your shoes.

The Hidden Tack

As you can imagine, pressing your toe against a tack, even fairly lightly, will cause a violent deflection in the polygraph needles. And if you suffer from ingrown toenails or blisters, you don't even need the tack; light pressure against the sore spot will achieve the same result. I even know of one person who deliberately cut his big toe the day before his test so that he didn't have to bother with the tack!

Biting the Tongue

Obviously, you should not try to bite your tongue while responding to a question. Immediately after you have answered, though, you should bite down hard for a few seconds and then release. Make sure to keep a straight face.

Shifting Positions

Shifting position in your chair can be tricky. You do not want to shift positions a number of times during the test (it looks like you're squirming). What you are trying to accomplish is a short, quick, unsuspicious shift. One technique is to begin the test by sitting up straight and then gradually leaning forward as the test progresses. When you get to a control question where you want to appear overly anxious, quickly shift so you are sitting up straight again. I would only try this once during the test because polygraphers are trained to be suspicious of anyone who exhibits a lot of extraneous physical motion.

Antiperspirant

There is some anecdotal evidence suggesting that a little antiperspirant on your fingertips will neutralize the GSR needle on the polygraph. This may be true, but don't go overboard with the antiperspirant. Remember, the polygrapher will be able to feel your fingertips when he applies the GSR electrodes. If he suspects you've doctored your fingertips, he may ask you to wash your hands before the test. Clear fingernail polish has been suggested as an alternative to antiperspirant, but it is much more easily detected.

Coughing, Sneezing, and Yawning

Don't waste your time with these. Everybody knows you can wipe out a polygraph test by coughing after every answer, but that would look a little ridiculous. Even if you try it only a few times, you still will not be getting away with anything. Any polygrapher worth his salt will make a notation on the chart whenever you cough, sneeze, or yawn, and he'll just disregard that response. What's more, if you cough or yawn a lot, the examiner will suspect that you are trying to pull a fast one on him and start looking for other indications that you may be using countermeasures.

APPLICATIONS OF PHYSICAL COUNTERMEASURES

With the R/I test, you are expected to show an elevated response to one or two relevant questions because everyone is assumed to have done things in their lives that they would rather not admit. The polygrapher will focus on these few areas for the remainder of the test. Your plan should be to use a physical countermeasure (that is, show an elevated response) on one or two questions about which you really have no worries. Your goal is to get the examiner to focus in on these areas and leave more potentially damaging areas of your life alone.

The CQT test is where your knowledge of question categories is all-important. You must be able to separate the control questions from the relevant questions and always show an elevated response to the control questions. *You cannot be judged deceptive if your responses to control questions are greater than or equal to your responses to relevant questions.* Never forget this.

Start by separating the control questions from the relevant questions during the pretest interview. When the test starts, sit calmly and breath regularly during all the relevant questions and use a countermeasure during all the control questions. You would be better off to use a series of different countermeasures so that your elevated responses don't have the same characteristics time after time. For example, try shallow breathing and a toe press during the first control question, pressing on a tack and a deep breath during the second, and biting the tongue hard and puckering the anus during the third.

Believe it or not, many polygraphers will only catch the most obvious and overt attempts at counter-measures. They simply do not expect you to have a sophisticated plan laid out in advance. This is a great advantage to you. As long as you don't get careless and sloppy, none but the very best examiners will have any idea that you've suckered them.

Because the GKT can only be used for specific incidence cases (i.e., after a crime has already been committed), innocent suspects don't need to learn any countermeasures. After all, an innocent person couldn't possibly know which items were filler and which were relevant. Consequently, as an innocent person, you are protected by this technique because 1) not knowing which items are relevant, you should show a fairly similar pattern of responses across all the items, and 2) even if you showed an elevated response to some of the items, it would be almost statistically impossible for you to coincidentally respond to enough critical items to put yourself in jeopardy. If you are guilty of a crime, however, then you need to know how to use these physical countermeasures to avoid being detected.

Some would argue that I shouldn't reveal this information because the guilty should be caught and punished. I have no desire to see thieves, muggers, rapists, and murderers getting off for crimes they have committed. My desire for revenge, however, is tempered by my desire to live in a world where people are not unjustly charged and convicted. I believe polygraph machines are unreliable and dangerous, and I hate to see one used to make a case for or against any person. If a person is indeed guilty, then there are more effective ways to prove it than charting how much he sweats or how rapidly he breathes.

That said, the best way I know of to neutralize a GKT exam is to dampen your responses to all of the items (see the sections on cognitive and pharmacological countermeasures), or to selectively elevate responses throughout the test. Because most GKT test questions have five or more alternatives, get a piece of paper and write the numbers 1 through 5 at the top of the page. Then write the numbers 1 through 10 in a column along the left-hand margin. Now, randomly choose one of the five numbers at the top and write it next to #1 in the left-hand column. An easy way to assure randomness is to roll a die and record whatever number comes up. If you roll a 6, just roll again.

Keep doing this until you have ten randomly chosen

numbers in the left-hand column. A typical sequence might be: 2, 5, 2, 4, 3, 5, 3, 4, 4, 1. Memorize this sequence. Then, when you are being tested, use the physical countermeasures to elevate whichever alternative is called for by your memorized sequence. If there are more than ten questions, just repeat the sequence over again until the test is finished; if there are less than ten questions, just start over at the beginning of your sequence for each repetition of the test.

The logic behind this technique is that you are imitating the thought processes of an innocent person by having elevated responses in an apparently random fashion. An innocent person couldn't possibly know which items are relevant, so his elevated responses should have no discernable pattern, and he stands a good chance of hitting at least one relevant alternative simply by coincidence. Your random sequence of numbers accomplishes the same thing. The only drawback to this technique is that it takes a lot of practice. I am confident, though, that the possibility of a prison term will serve as ample motivation.

COGNITIVE COUNTERMEASURES

Unlike physical countermeasures, cognitive countermeasures are impossible to detect—even by the most experienced examiners. As mentioned earlier, the polygrapher is relying on your ignorance and gullibility and expects your driving motivation is to tell the truth. When you use a cognitive countermeasure, telling the truth becomes secondary to altering the way in which you perceive the test.

Hypnosis/Biofeedback
The jury is still out about the effectiveness of hypnosis and biofeedback to appreciably alter a polygraph test's results. Some say hypnotic suggestion

(e.g., hypnotically suggested amnesia) is an effective countermeasure. Others say it is just a waste of time. Biofeedback, on the other hand, has long been used to lower blood pressure and ease stress. Hard-driving Type A personalities, whose lives are characterized by stress, are especially receptive to the calming effects of biofeedback. This has led some researchers to theorize that biofeedback might also help to lower blood pressure in normal individuals during specific stressful situations (such as a lie detector test).

The research in this area looks promising. In fact, subjects have been taught not only how to lower their blood pressure, but how to significantly lower their GSR levels as well. That's two out of three of the major physiological measures used in a polygraph exam! The only drawback to biofeedback (and hypnosis) is that it costs a lot of money and takes a lot of practice to achieve any measurable reductions. One alternative would be to invest in one of the relatively low-cost biofeedback monitors advertised in high-tech mail order catalogs and the backs of magazines (*Psychology Today* and all the new age and health magazines usually run at least one ad for this type of equipment every month). There is no reason you shouldn't be able to get the same results at home as others who have spent a fortune on high-priced clinical workshops.

Thought Control

No, this does not refer to some covert CIA operation. Thought control is simply an individual's conscious effort to alter his or her perceptions of reality. Once again, the ability to differentiate between the three question categories is essential. The basic procedure is to dissociate yourself from the relevant questions and heighten your response to the control questions. For example, when the polygrapher asks you the relevant question, "Did you steal the three hundred dollars from the cash register," you would concentrate on peaceful thoughts like the crashing surf, a lazy Sunday afternoon on the lake, or anything else that takes your mind off the question.

Alternatively, when asked a relevant question, you can convince yourself that the question means something other than what was intended. The question "Have you ever consumed alcoholic beverages while on the job" could, for example, be rationalized as follows: "Well, I have been hiding a bottle of whiskey in the rest room and drinking it there . . . but when I'm in the rest room I'm not really 'on the job' . . . so no, I've never consumed alcoholic beverages while on the job." Responses to control questions could similarly be elevated by disregarding the question and focusing on stressful thoughts like what would happen if you were to lose your job, go to jail, total your car on the way home, be audited by the IRS, and so on.

To date, only one researcher has attempted to test this technique. In a laboratory study of polygraph examinations, this researcher recruited a group of method actors from his school's drama department and told them that they should apply their acting skills to appear innocent during the polygraph exam. Every actor was detected. This was not really a fair experiment, however, because the design was flawed. You see, the experimenter had only told the drama students to *act* innocent during the polygraph exam. He had not given them any training about how to tailor their responses to particular questions or about how a polygraph exam goes about detecting deception. With the knowledge you have already accumulated, you would stand a much better chance against a trained polygraph examiner than any of these method actors.

Results Feedback

It has long been proven that school children will make better grades on weekly tests if they know how they did on the previous week's test. The same seems to be true for polygraph exams. If you have had to undergo polygraph exams in the past and you were not judged deceptive, you stand a better chance of passing future polygraph exams than someone who has never taken one. Remember when your parents told you that practice makes perfect? Here's another example that shows they were right.

Belief in the Machine

The final cognitive countermeasure is really a frame of mind or pattern of thinking that underlies everything else in this book: belief in, or skepticism toward, the machine. If you believe the polygraph machine can detect your deceptions, it will. If, on the other hand, you are confident that the polygraph machine is no more able to weed out lies than snake oil can cure cancer, you will avoid detection. Several university researchers have accumulated evidence supporting this theory by conducting what is known as "bogus pipeline" research.

Bogus pipeline theory proposes that when subjects believe that their attitudes are detectable by a physiological recording device, they more readily express their actual attitudes. The problem facing the university researchers was to convince the skeptical college student that the polygraph machine actually works. They accomplished this by presenting the subject with an impressive display of electronic gadgetry and promoting it as a new kind of super lie detector capable of detecting even the smallest physiological changes. ("Bogus pipeline" refers to all the wires, relays, and displays that are purportedly used to detect deception. In reality, all this sophisticated gadgetry has nothing to do with lie detection—it is intended to intimidate the subject. All style, no substance.) Subjects deceived in this way have been found to admit to more socially undesirable responses, such as negative attitudes toward handicapped people. The researchers claim these confessions are evidence that the bogus pipeline can bring about a higher level of "truthfulness."

The significance of this research for our purpose is that if the validity of polygraph testing is dependent upon the subject's belief in the effectiveness of the machine, then a possible countermeasure would involve training people to believe that the polygraph does not work. Simply put, your goal is to go into the exam with the utmost skepticism. The more dubious you are of the polygrapher's claims, the more difficult it will be for him to trip you up.

APPLICATIONS OF COGNITIVE COUNTERMEASURES

Your best defense against the R/I Technique is to go into the exam with the strongest possible belief that the machine doesn't work and cannot harm you. You can supplement this by thinking peaceful thoughts during the relevant questions that concern you and thinking stressful thoughts on one or two relevant questions that do not cause you any concern. Your goal is to get the examiner to shift the focus of the test to those areas about which you are not really worried. Once you see him moving in that direction, however, you stop elevating your responses and begin thinking peaceful thoughts again.

As mentioned before, the way to beat a CQT is to elevate your responses to control questions and attenuate your responses to relevant questions. Once again, you need to go into the test with the proper frame of mind (i.e., skepticism) and use the peaceful thoughts/stressful thoughts technique discussed above. You can also try hypnosis and biofeedback if you are so inclined and have the money.

For the GKT, innocent suspects don't need countermeasures. Guilty persons, on the other hand, may want to seriously consider all the cognitive countermeasures available. Should you use the controlling thoughts countermeasure, apply the random numbers sequence discussed under physiological countermeasures. This time, however, think stressful thoughts whenever the preselected random alternative comes up and try to dissociate yourself from all the other alternatives presented. Practicing with a biofeedback monitor would help you assess how quickly you can switch from a peaceful to a stressful frame of mind and back again.

PHARMACOLOGICAL COUNTERMEASURES

In contrast to physical countermeasures, which may be detected by an observant polygraph examiner (either by noticing unusual behaviors or running multiple polygraph charts), the use of various pharmacological agents, or drugs, may be more difficult to detect. The downside of these techniques is that current research on the effectiveness of drug countermeasures is not very promising. In fact, ingesting a drug before you take a polygraph exam may be the worst thing you can do. Douglas Gene Williams, a former Oklahoma police polygrapher who since 1978 has conducted a personal campaign against lie detectors, advises anyone who is about to take a polygraph exam to stay away from drugs. He argues that you need to keep your wits about you during an examination—drugs will only dull your senses and cause you to become confused and make mistakes.

Some of you, however, have probably heard

fantastic tales about how someone took some miracle drug and passed a lie detector test with flying colors. There are some substances that may help.

Warning: The following section on drug usage is *for information purposes only.* Neither the publisher nor the author encourages or endorses the use of drugs or other controlled substances without a proper prescription. Some of the drugs listed may have dangerous and even life-threatening side effects. Consult a physician before attempting to use any of these medications.

The drugs most commonly used to escape detection are the classical sedatives and a special class of tranquilizers called ataractics. As their name implies, sedatives are calming agents that allay anxiety and lower the level of tension. The major drawback of sedatives is that they are nonselective: not only do they lower autonomic responses (GSR, blood pressure, breathing rate), but they also affect overt psychomotor behaviors. In other words, the subject's responses on the polygraph chart would flatten out, but so would the subject himself. Concentration would be reduced, reaction time would be slowed, and a mild hypnotic effect would most likely be experienced. These symptoms are easy to spot, and no polygrapher in the world would administer a polygraph exam to someone who appeared to be doped up. That brings us to the ataractics.

Ataractics are compounds with a tranquilizing effect, which is to say they are sedative in nature. But the influence of ataractics is limited more to the subcortical systems (more specifically, the reticular formation, which controls the sleep/wake cycle) and the limbic system. Consequently, unlike classic sedatives, ataractics will have little influence on clarity of consciousness and intellectual performance. In other words, the subject's autonomic nervous system will be mildly sedated, but he or she won't appear to be doped up to the examiner.

Commonly Prescribed Ataractics

GENERIC NAME: Chlordiazepoxide hydrochloride

CATEGORY: Schedule IV controlled substance

COMMON BRAND NAMES: Librium, Corax, Libritabs, Protensin, Sereen, Tenax, Zetran

DOSAGE: Daily oral dose is 10-50 mg.

ONSET AND DURATION: 1-2 hours onset; up to 24-hour duration

SIDE EFFECTS: Lethargy, nausea, abdominal discomfort, transient hypotension (low blood pressure)

PARTICULARS: Chlordiazepoxide was introduced in clinical psychiatry in 1960. Its side effects after oral administration are slight, but it may cause psychomotor weakness. This drug should never be taken with alcohol, and it is not recommended for day-to-day use.

GENERIC NAME: Diazepam

CATEGORY: Schedule IV controlled substance

COMMON BRAND NAMES: Valium, Levium, Stesoloid, D-Tran, Erital

DOSAGE: Daily oral dose is 6-30 mg.

ONSET AND DURATION: 1 hour onset, up to 24-hour duration

SIDE EFFECTS: Lethargy, nausea, abdominal discomfort, transient hypotension

PARTICULARS: Diazepam has a more marked sedative and hypnotic effect than chlordiazepoxide. Intense drowsiness can be a problem, especially when it is taken for the first time. Although easily available, diazepam is not a good choice for a pharmacological countermeasure. It is likely to cause drowsiness, clumsiness, or slurred speech, which will quickly tip off a competent polygraph examiner that a subject is under the influence of some drug.

GENERIC NAME: Meprobamate

CATEGORY: Schedule IV controlled substance

COMMON BRAND NAMES: Equanil, Miltown, Sedapon, Arcoban, Meribam, Saronil

DOSAGE: Varies widely. The average daily dose is 400-1200 mg., but doses up to 2-3 grams are tolerated.

ONSET AND DURATION: Begins therapeutic action in 1 hour; peaks in 2-3 hours; half-life of about 10 hours

SIDE EFFECTS: Drowsiness, dizziness, slurred speech, headache, hypotension, nausea, palpitations

PARTICULARS: Prior to the introduction of chlordiazepoxide, meprobamate was by far the most popular ataractic. It derives from mephenesin, a compound introduced as a muscle relaxant shortly after World War II. When it was found that mephenesin had sedative properties as well, efforts were made to alter the molecule so that duration and intensity of the sedative effect were enhanced. Meprobamate was the result. Meprobamate is one of the few drugs to be scientifically tested and found to reduce the accuracy of polygraph examiners' judgments (Waid, Orne, Cook, and Orne, 1981).

GENERIC NAME: Propanolol

CATEGORY: Schedule IV controlled substance

COMMON BRAND NAMES: Inderal

DOSAGE: Daily dose is 40-160 mg.

ONSET AND DURATION: Can act as quickly as 1-5 minutes and have a 6-24 hour duration

SIDE EFFECTS: Fatigue, lethargy, hallucinations, hypotension, nausea, skin rash

PARTICULARS: Propanolol falls into a special class of ataractics known as beta-blockers. Though normally prescribed for hypertension, propanolol has also been found to be useful in combating incidental tensions produced by anticipation of stressful events (e.g., a midterm exam, a speech, a polygraph test). This drug is particularly effective when anxiety is manifested in somatic symptoms (e.g., heart palpitations, nausea, diarrhea). Beta-blockers are quickly gaining a solid reputation as reliable pharmacological counter-measures.

GENERIC NAME: Atenolol
CATEGORY: Schedule IV controlled substance
COMMON BRAND NAMES: Tenormin
DOSAGE: Daily dose is 50-100 mg.
ONSET AND DURATION: Can act as quickly as 1-5 minutes and have a 6-24 hour duration
SIDE EFFECTS: Fatigue, lethargy, hallucinations, hypotension, nausea, skin rash, fever
PARTICULARS: Atenolol is a relatively new beta-blocker, but it is also commonly prescribed for individuals with transitory stage fright or performance anxiety. Other beta-blockers have also been found effective in anxiety syndromes with a strong somatic component. Two commonly prescribed medications are alprenolol (Aptine) and oxprenolol (Trasicor). The last compound, given in a single 40-mg. dose, has helped many professional actors overcome extreme cases of opening night jitters.

Getting the Drugs

Once again, I cannot stress enough that you should see a doctor if you want to try to use any of these drugs as polygraph countermeasures. Unfortunately, many conservative doctors may not want to prescribe a drug for you just so that you can beat a lie detector test. Therefore, you must have a good reason for needing the drug. Your best bet would probably be to tell your doctor that you have a major college exam coming up or that you have to make a major presentation in front of a large audience. Then tell him that in the past, you have gotten heart palpitations, nausea, and diarrhea whenever you had to face such a situation. Being able to present the doctor with a list of physical components such as this is a must; if you only tell him that you "feel nervous," he may think you're overreacting and prescribe a placebo. A doctor will be much more likely to prescribe medication for "heart palpitations" than for "a nervous feeling."

Applying Pharmacological Countermeasures

Whether the polygraph exam is of the R/I, CQT, or GKT variety, the only way to apply a pharmacological countermeasure is to take the drug before the exam and hope for the best. All of the drugs outlined above will tend to flatten out physiological responses, which may or may not help. One likely outcome is that the test will be judged inconclusive and have to be taken some other time. In some instances, however, an inconclusive result is viewed as a *de facto* pass, and the test will not have to be taken again.

CONCLUSIONS

Despite what the polygraph industry would have you believe, physical, cognitive, and pharmacological countermeasures are effective means of neutralizing most polygraph examinations. The risk of being caught is minimal, and the rewards for success can be substantial (like keeping yourself out of jail).

If you never want to fear another polygraph exam, you must do two things: 1) learn how to differentiate between relevant questions, irrelevant questions, and control questions; and 2) *practice, practice, practice.* Pick out a few of the countermeasures that appeal to you and practice carrying them out without looking obvious. Then, get a friend and run through the sample tests at the end of Chapter 4. Make the situation as real as possible and have your friend look for any telltale signs of countermeasures that you may have missed.

The better you get in practice, the better you'll do if and when you have to undergo the real thing.

CHAPTER SIX

THE DAY OF THE TEST

"Any fool can tell the truth, but it requires a man of some sense to know how to lie well."

—Samuel Butler

As with a dentist's appointment, a trip to a polygrapher's office is something most people dread. If you've ever had to take a polygraph exam, then you know the feelings that precede it: anxiety over not knowing what to expect, resentment over having to submit to such a procedure in the first place, and outright anger over the possibility that some stranger may brand you a liar. These feelings are quite normal, and you have every right to express them. But when you do, make sure it is only to friends and family, not to the polygrapher. All the adverse feelings you have toward either the machine or the examiner should be left at the front door when you leave your home in the morning.

BEFORE YOU LEAVE FOR THE EXAM

Put yourself in the proper mind-set for the ordeal that lies ahead. There are several things you should do to prepare yourself emotionally and psychologically.

Clothing is always important. Consider the following: A young man was arrested late one Friday evening for possession of marijuana. At the time of the arrest, the police officers had a great time making fun of his long, greasy hair, tie-dyed T-shirt, and dirty, torn blue jeans. But by the time his hearing came up, his entire appearance had changed. The hair was trimmed short and styled to perfection, and the tie-dyed shirt and blue jeans had given way to a three-piece Brooks Brothers suit. Obviously, someone (probably his lawyer) had told him that people who dress like bums are often discriminated against, but everyone forgives a clean-cut youth.

You should try to dress nicely for the exam. Rest assured that the examiner will be doing everything in his power to impart to you a professional demeanor. Men should wear a jacket and tie and remember to shave. Women should wear a tailored suit or skirt and blouse. Keep jewelry to a minimum and be conservative with makeup. T-shirts, jeans, tennis shoes, shorts, and jogging suits or sweats are definite no-no's. The whole idea is to take away any psychological advantage the examiner may have over you by being more professionally dressed. When choosing your outfit, you may want to go with loose fitting—not baggy—clothes (the better to conceal muscle flexing) and nonsqueaky shoes (and don't forget to hide the tack in your sock).

The last thing you should do before you leave for the exam is to take a brief inventory of your polygraph skills. Remember the four types of polygraph questions: relevant, irrelevant, control, guilty knowledge. Be certain you can differentiate between them. Go over the three polygraph exam techniques. Review your countermeasures. Do you have a "game plan" for their use? All of these things are important, and you should be able to recall all of them without hesitation. Remember—the polygraph examiner does this every day. You've got only one shot, so make the most of it.

ARRIVING AT THE EXAM LOCATION

Whether your exam is conducted at your place of employment, a downtown office building, a police station, or even in a hotel room, the cardinal rule is *be on time!* I cannot stress this enough. Your examiner will automatically interpret any lateness as a conscious or subconscious attempt to avoid or delay the test. Being late is a surefire way to raise suspicions in the examiner about some presumed hidden motives, so don't let him put a black mark beside your name before you even show up. If you are not sure of where the testing site is, make a few dry runs before the actual day of the test. Is there adequate parking? Will the early-morning rush hour or the lunchtime traffic snarls delay your arrival? Any lateness, no matter how small and no matter how unintentional or unavoidable, will be the first strike against you.

If you are lucky, your polygraph exam will be conducted either at your place of employment or in a hotel room. In the former case, the examiner is off his home turf and in surroundings with which you are more familiar. In the latter case, the turf is fairly neutral. He may be the one renting the room (a small psychological advantage), but hotel rooms are, by and large, nonthreatening, and you can get your own psychological edge by pointing out (gently) that a hotel room seems like a strange place to be doing such "important" testing. This puts the examiner on the defensive immediately, because by noting the peculiarity of the surroundings, you have indirectly commented on his professionalism. No doubt he will try to save face by explaining to you that his office is being painted or that he has chosen this location for your benefit so that you don't have to drive so far. No matter what reason he gives, all he is trying to do is convince you that he is a professional and that the atypical surroundings will have no effect on the testing process.

If, on the other hand, your exam is conducted at a police station or in the polygrapher's office, then you are automatically at a disadvantage. You are on his turf, and he has probably manipulated the surroundings to make himself look like the ultimate professional. Don't be surprised to see a wall full of diplomas, certificates of achievement, awards, and so on, testifying to his abilities. This is a subtle psychological ploy often used by "professionals." A framed diploma is an excellent way for someone to say, "See how great I am" without uttering a word.

Another item you may notice in the office is an American flag. Ronald Reagan proved (as if there were ever any doubt) that you can get away with just about anything by wrapping yourself in the flag. A flag in the polygrapher's office subconsciously sends the message, "This guy is an American. He believes in American values and would never do anything to subvert your constitutionally protected rights." If you would like to counter this little patriotic ploy, fight fire with fire. Show up for the test wearing a little American flag lapel pin.

If your polygrapher is a prominent one, then you may expect to spend some time in an outer office before the pretest interview begins. While you are waiting, don't sit there and fidget or stare blindly into space. Why? Because that fancy office probably has a one-way mirror disguised as a picture or even a fish tank. The polygrapher will be observing you from the moment you enter the office, looking for inadvertent signs of deceptiveness. Don't give him any. Keep yourself busy.

One of the best defenses is to bring something with you to read. More importantly, bring something to read that makes you look like someone to be treated with respect. Ask yourself, "Would I be more impressed if I saw a stranger in a waiting room reading Stephen Hawking's *A Brief History of Time* or a tabloid bearing the headline, "The Government Took My UFO Baby!" A local newspaper is always a good choice; *The Wall Street Journal* would be even better. Most current magazines would be all right (except for gossipy ones like *People* or *Us*). A professional journal or current bestseller would be better. No steamy romance novels, no potboilers, no pulp westerns, no tabloids, no comic books. And for God's sake, don't bring this book. You just want to have something with you to fill the time before your test begins. You don't really have to read what you bring, but you should go through the motions. (Remember, you're being watched.)

MEETING THE EXAMINER

Attitude is the key. Don't greet the examiner with a sarcastic remark like, "So, you're gonna try to read my mind, huh?" Your initial contact should exude friendliness. A firm (not vicelike) handshake coupled with a sincere and confident personal introduction will go a long way. I know it sounds corny to say you never get a second chance to make a first impression, but it's true. Psychologists know about the benefits of favorable first impressions, and you should too.

The "halo effect" refers to the tendency of individuals to allow their general initial impressions of others to distort their overall judgments about them. This effect has been gauged in a number of experimental settings, and the results have been fairly uniform. In a typical university study, college students watched one of two videotapes of a college instructor. In one, the instructor acted in a warm and friendly manner. In the other, he appeared cold and aloof. After watching one of the two tapes, the students were asked to rate the examiner on friendliness, physical appearance, mannerisms, and accent (he was Belgian). As expected, the warm versus the cold variables affected the subjects' responses significantly. Those who had seen the instructor behave in a warm manner reported liking him much more than those who had seen him behave in a cold fashion. Of greater interest was the amount of "spillover" from these global reactions to his individual traits. Students who had seen him behave in a cold manner and who formed a negative impression of him also rated his mannerisms, appearance, and accent as unfavorable, and vice versa.

After completing their ratings, some students were asked whether the instructor's friendliness had affected their ratings of his appearance, mannerisms, and accent. Surprisingly, the students overwhelmingly rejected this idea. But when other students were asked whether they felt the instructor's appearance, mannerisms, and accent had affected their overall ratings of his friendliness, a number of them said yes.

These findings suggest that the students' view of the process was totally reversed. Clearly, they were unaware of the influence the halo effect had on them. The halo effect can result from anything that produces a positive or negative impression. A person can be regarded favorably because of being an outstanding athlete, a great scholar, a powerful business executive, a warm family member, or purely because he or she is physically attractive. The tendency is to perceive all of a person's characteristics as favorable so that they are consistent with the initial overall impression. Unfortunately, the reverse is also true. For example, it is common to perceive an overweight person or one who is of an unpopular race or nationality as having other negative characteristics as well.

With this in mind, you should certainly greet the polygraph examiner in a friendly manner in the hope this will generate nothing but positive thoughts in his mind. This process continues as he leads you into the examination area, sits you down, and prepares to begin the technical portion of the pretest interview. During this time, the two of you will probably discuss the weather, sports, or other nonthreatening subjects. Remember, the examiner not only wants you to relax, he also wants you to dispel any negative feelings you may have toward him. He realizes his is not a popular profession and that many people think he is a bully or a monster. By setting a relaxed and easy tone at the outset, he wants to manipulate your attitudes and get you in the proper mind-set.

THE PRETEST INTERVIEW

Technically, the pretest interview begins when the examiner first meets you. It is a process during which each party sizes up the other. Some prominent polygraphers have stated that the pretest interview is *the* most important part of the whole procedure. Basically, its purpose is twofold: 1) to provide you with information about the examination and inform you of your legal rights, and 2) to persuade you that the examination is conducted professionally and that any attempts at deception will be painfully obvious. At this point, guilty suspects are supposed to recognize the confidence in the examiner's voice and start to get anxious. Innocent suspects, on the other hand, are supposed to trust in the examiner's display of confidence and be less anxious.

The pretest also allows the examiner to assess any special conditions or circumstances that may affect physiological responsiveness. You should therefore expect questions about medical problems as well as drugs you may be taking that could influence autonomic responding (obviously, you should not mention drugs you may have ingested for countermeasure purposes). Although it is highly unlikely that an examiner will ask you to submit a blood sample, you might have to give a urine sample. Not to worry, though. Most urine testing labs will only screen for illegal drugs (e.g., marijuana, cocaine, heroin, etc.), so there is a good possibility that the ataractics described in the previous chapter won't show up.

If, however, you are unfortunate enough to have your sample sent to a really good lab and the ataractics are detected, there is no need to panic. All of the drugs outlined earlier are antihypertensives, so you could say that you were taking them for high blood pressure. If anyone asks you why you didn't tell the polygrapher about this medication, you can say that you had stopped taking the drug before the exam, and anything found in your sample must have just been a residual amount.

Once the small talk and pleasantries are over with and all the prerequisite information has been obtained, the examiner will get down to the real nuts and bolts of the pretest interview: convincing you of the polygraph's validity and formulating his questions. These two processes go on simultaneously. He will sound very confident and authoritative and will probably have well-rehearsed answers for the most commonly asked questions:

1. How accurate is the machine?
2. I hear these things are not conclusive.

3. Can't you beat these machines pretty easily?

4. Why should I trust that machine to make such an important determination?

5. Why do I have to take this test? I didn't do anything wrong.

6. What's the point in taking this test if it won't even hold up in court?

I wouldn't advise you to get into an argument with the examiner over any of these questions. If you get into a protracted debate with him, you will lose all that good will you have been trying to build. I recommend that you play the role he wants you to play during the pretest interview. Ask some questions, but don't be too skeptical. Unless you're a hermit, you have heard about polygraph exams from friends, coworkers, newspapers, or television. The polygrapher expects this. In fact, he wants you to ask questions about the procedure so he can gauge how much you know about the machine and how you feel about the process.

The trick here is to ask questions about polygraphs without sounding like a smartass or a know-it-all. There is a wrong way and a right way to ask a question. "Aren't these machines really pretty easy to beat?" is an example of the wrong way. First of all, this implies that polygraph exams aren't trustworthy and that polygraph examiners aren't capable of catching people who cheat. In only eight short words, you have managed to trash the man, his chosen occupation, and the industry as a whole. This is not the way to stay on his good side. Secondly, and perhaps more importantly, this question implies deception. The examiner may come right back at you with, "The only people I know who have to 'beat' a test are those who really have something to hide. Do you fall into that category?" Don't get caught in this trap! Think before you speak!

A much better form of this question would be,

"Someone told me about tricks you can use to make sure that you pass one of these, but they really don't work, do they?" You are making the same point, but you have softened it so the examiner will not feel you are challenging his authority. More importantly, by asking the examiner to confirm your "doubts" about countermeasures, you have shown him you are willing to bow down to the superiority of the machine. Polygraphers love a question like this because it implies that you think polygraph examinations really work, and it allows them to boost their egos by confirming your suspicions with a bunch of pseudotechnical jargon.

Pump the examiner up. Flatter him. But don't go too far. It can backfire if you start to gush all over him. Stay away from compliments about his clothes or overall appearance—they always sound phony. If you really want to stroke him, comment on his diplomas and certificates. Say something like, "I didn't know polygraphy took so much training. It must have taken you a long time to earn (always say 'earn'—never 'get') all of these." Done correctly, this phrase should imply a genuine admiration for your examiner's commitment to his profession. Another good ego booster is to pretend you've heard of the polygraph school named on his diploma. Say something like, "That's supposed to be a pretty good school, isn't it? I had a friend who was talking about going there." This demonstrates that you have respect for his profession (you can enjoy the quiet irony of lying through your teeth later).

Don't act like you are "above" this sort of thing. Once again, you run into the problem of downgrading the examiner's profession. You may believe (as I do) that polygraph exams are nothing more than electronic voodoo—a simplistic attempt to rectify such complex problems as employee turnover, theft, and drug abuse without spending the money to get the job done right.

Most polygraphers, however, are sincere in their belief that they provide a valuable service. You should not, therefore, walk into the examining room with a bad attitude. You may very well feel hurt or embarrassed or even outraged that you have to submit to such a test, but keep it to yourself. The fragile relationship you have developed with the examiner will stay on a friendly course if you can convince him that you, too, are dismayed at all the dishonesty in the workplace and realize that polygraph exams have become a necessary tool for weeding out thieves. Simply put, if he thinks you respect his profession, he may be more apt to give you the benefit of the doubt should your chart data fall right on the borderline between deceptiveness and nondeceptiveness.

It's very important to express confidence that you'll pass the test. As the pretest interview draws to a close, the examiner will have mentally labeled you as a skeptic or a believer, a troublemaker or a team player. Polygraphers frown on skeptics but enjoy the psychological control they feel they exert over believers. Naturally, you want to be seen as a believer. Get enthusiastic about the test and let the examiner know that you have absolute confidence in his abilities. Express a positive attitude that the exam will prove your innocence once and for all. By exhibiting this attitude, you are confirming to the examiner that he has done his job well—all your questions have been answered, all doubts cleared up. In his eyes, you have become the ideal examinee.

The typical ending to the pretest interview (which can last from twenty to ninety minutes or longer) consists of a final review of the test questions and a request that you sign a consent form. By this time, you should have a firm idea of which questions are controls and which ones are relevant, and the examiner should have them all listed on paper. If he doesn't show you this list of questions voluntarily, ask to see it. If he hesitates, complain (gently) that you want to make sure that there are no unfair or improper questions. Almost all professional examiners will allow you to look at the list, but don't expect to find a big heading labeled RELEVANTS and a big heading labeled CONTROLS. You will have to pick those out yourself.

Fortunately, it is against the polygraph industry's rules to ask any question that does not come from this list. Therefore, once you have familiarized yourself with the controls and relevants on the page, you won't have to fear some kind of surprise question pulled out of nowhere. That kind of trick is really frowned upon by the industry and can be used as grounds for invalidating the whole test.

Once these details are cleared up, the examiner will ask you to give your voluntary consent to be tested. Consent procedures vary depending on the nature of the interview, the most important differences being between tests given for criminal investigations and tests given for preemployment screening.

If the exam is conducted as part of a criminal investigation, you should be read a copy of your Miranda rights and then be told that the exam is completely voluntary. You should also be informed whether or not the examination will be observed from outside the room or recorded or videotaped. Normally, all these specifications are typed up and you are asked to sign at the bottom. Applicants for employment need not be advised of their right to speak with an attorney but may, depending on local laws, be advised that the test is voluntary. In the case of such employment-related tests, along with a provision concerning voluntary consent, you should be told how the results of the examination will be used. For example, you may be informed that a copy of the test results will be provided to the sponsor of the exam (i.e., your prospective employer), that you have a right to obtain a personal copy of the test results, and that you will not be asked any questions regarding political or religious affiliations, union activities, or sexual activities unless these areas are specifically related to the issue under investigation.

Treat cautiously any statement or paragraph that may seem to limit your legal rights. Some consent forms contain a section that protects the test sponsor or the polygrapher (or both) from liability. If yours has such a statement and you sign it, you may be waiving your rights to any future legal action. You should *never* sign a consent form like this unless and until you see a lawyer. Undoubtedly, the polygrapher will accuse you of overreacting or trying to hide something, but don't let him trick you. The only reason he wants you to sign such a statement is to keep from being sued! Believe it or not, polygraphers are being sued successfully by an increasing number of disgruntled individuals whose polygraph test results have had an adverse impact on their lives. Like doctors, polygraphers are having to purchase malpractice insurance. So don't let some smooth-talking polygrapher goad you into signing a waiver of your rights. He's not looking out for you; he's looking out for himself.

TESTING

So far, you have presented a charming, friendly, pleasant, flattering, and ingratiating personality. Now, however, you need to focus on the task at hand: beating the test. The actual polygraph test is relatively brief, and each examiner probably conducts his test in a slightly different way. But the general order of events is as follows.

Hooking Up

If you are not seated there already, the polygrapher

will place you in the examination chair. It will most likely be placed alongside the examiner's desk so that when you are seated he will be looking at your profile (or the back of your head) and you will be looking, most likely, at a wall. The polygraph machine and its attachments will be lying on top of the desk. First, the pneumograph tube will be placed around your chest. Some examiners will use two tubes and will place one around your chest and one around your stomach. Second, electrodes will be attached to your fingertips (in some cases electrode jelly will be applied to your fingertips to increase conductivity). Third, the sphygmomanometer will be placed around your arm and inflated slightly so that the machine can get a good cardio reading.

Ideally, this entire process should take less than a minute. Believe me, it can seem like a long minute. All polygraphers know that this hooking up process is a great fear inducer, and they will be paying particular attention to anything you say or do while the attachments are made. Therefore, don't get cute and make offhand remarks like "electric chair," "I'm in the hot seat now," "How soon till blast-off," or "Have you heard from the governor?" While it is a natural human reaction to make jokes in times of stress, the polygrapher may interpret them as indications of your guilt. The best thing to do is sit quietly and try to relax. If you are lucky, the examiner will give a running explanation of what each attachment is used for as it is applied. If he doesn't, ask questions. Concentrate on his words. Continue to exude an air of anxious optimism. That way you aren't just sitting there stewing.

The Stim Test: The Ultimate Deception
After you are hooked up, the examiner will begin recording physiological baseline measurements. Don't

be alarmed if these initial tracings look pretty damaging. This is natural and is called an "orienting response." Basically, an orienting response can be thought of as a natural tendency to show elevated responsiveness to any new stimulus. When referring to a polygraph exam, the orienting response is that initial anxiety you feel over actually being hooked up and having your autonomic responses recorded. This will subside eventually, and the examiner will watch the charts to get a clear indication of your normal level of arousal. When he is satisfied that he has enough baseline readings, he will most likely carry out what is known in the business as a stimulation or "stim" test.

Stim tests are designed to show even the most skeptical person that the polygraph machine can really differentiate between the truth and deception. It starts innocently enough: the examiner will ask you to pick a standard playing card from a group of cards or to choose a card from a special pack of numbered cards. In one version, the examiner will ask you not to reveal what the card (or the number) is, but to simply concentrate on it. He will then ask you a series of questions so as to determine what card or number was selected. This line of questioning will go something like, "Was it a spade? Was it a face card? Was it a black card? Was it the King of Spades?" Rest assured, he will be able to tell you which card you selected. What he will not reveal to you is that you have been conned. The deck of cards he used was probably marked, or the cards may have been laid out on the table in such a way that he can tell what card you selected simply from its position in the deck. Either way, he knew what card you selected even before you did.

The whole rigmarole of asking you questions about your card is what magicians call misdirection: a deliberate attempt to direct your attention away from how the trick is really done. Is this deception really necessary? Well, yes and no. Actually, the polygrapher could figure out what card you selected without cheating, but that method is unreliable. Studies have shown that, based entirely on polygraph tracings, experienced examiners can correctly identify the chosen card up to 73 percent of the time. That figure, however, is not good enough for a polygraph test. Since the object of the stim test is to convince the subject that the polygraph can determine when deception is occurring, being correct only one-half to three-quarters of the time is not good enough. The need to be accurate 100 percent of the time requires examiners to cheat.

An alternate form of the stim test does not involve outright cheating by the examiner, but trickery is still involved. In this version, the examiner will ask you to pick a number from 1 to 10 and write it down where you can both see it. Next, he will instruct you to say "no" to each question of the form, "Did you write down number_____?" He will say that this is a procedure used to calibrate the machine so that he will have a clear indication of what your tracings look like when you tell the truth as opposed to when you lie. This statement is, of course, untrue and misleading, but the examiner will no doubt make a big production out of tearing the chart from the machine, showing you your tracings, and pointing out where you were lying.

Lots of people get taken in by these theatrics, and studies have shown that "successfully administered" stim tests can increase the validity of the polygraph exam (Senese, *Journal of Police Science and Administration*, 1976). If you know in advance that the polygrapher will be playing these little mind games with you, you will not be as likely to give the examiner credit when none is deserved.

The Real Test
After impressing you with his magic tricks during

the stim test, the examiner is ready to proceed with the real thing. The test will begin with a fifteen- to twenty-second (or longer) pause to allow your responses to return to baseline levels. A fifteen- to twenty-second pause will also follow each question, allowing time for the previous response to fade and the physiological measures to return to baseline. This procedure is followed throughout the test, with the examiner carefully noting on the chart when the test began, when questions were asked, and when the test ended. Any extraneous behaviors such as coughing, sneezing, or shifting positions in the chair are also noted. After the entire set of questions is asked, that particular test ends, and the examiner will usually deflate the blood pressure cuff so as not to cause you any undue physical discomfort. He may then ask for clarifications on certain questions or make other refinements, and then he will repeat the test two or three more times to give the examiner three to four charts from which he will render his opinion.

Don't be surprised if the examiner is called away from the room during testing. This is another common trick—to make you sweat it out alone with your thoughts and let your anxiety build. You should also expect this room to be equipped with one-way mirrors or listening devices (remember the consent form you signed?), so watch yourself. Don't fidget, don't try to look at your chart, and don't start talking to yourself. It is best to act nonchalant or even bored, and if you brought your reading material in with you, by all means, start reading. This will indicate to the examiner that you are not afraid of the test and have nothing to hide.

The Post-Test Interrogation

The final component of the examination is the post-test interrogation. If you're lucky, you may not have to go through this part of the process. If, up to this point, the examiner believes you are being truthful, and if this view seems to be confirmed by a lack of strong physiological reaction to the relevant questions, then the final interrogation may be dispensed with. The polygrapher will tell you that he could find no indications of deception on your part and that he will say as much when he makes his report to the test sponsor. Consider yourself lucky—you have just passed your polygraph exam.

If, on the other hand, the polygrapher thinks you are being deceptive, then you have another ordeal to endure—the post-test interrogation. The examiner will remove the polygraph attachments, seat himself facing you—toe-to-toe, knee-to-knee, and face-to-face—and make an opening remark like, "I think you've got a problem." For many polygraphers, the post-test interrogation and the confession it often induces is the object of the whole examination. Some long-time polygraphers even admit that they don't care whether the test is valid or not; they only go through the process so they will have enough ammunition to elicit (coerce?) a confession during the interrogation.

Many researchers, including Lykken (1981) and Budiansky (1984), believe this is one of the most dangerous aspects of a polygraph exam because a naive suspect who is judged deceptive could be tricked or bullied into making a false confession. You should *never* confess to *anything* during the post-test interrogation or, for that matter, at any other time before, during, or after the test. If you confess, the polygrapher has won. He has earned his pay. You, on the other hand, have admitted your guilt and solved everyone's problems. Remember, the results of a polygraph exam are not proof of anything. Even if you fail the test with flying colors, what has that proved? If you ask me, it only proves that you suffered from a lot of anxiety during the examination and didn't respond the way that this "professional" thought you should. In my mind, there is still a great amount of doubt that you are guilty of the incident under investigation. But when you confess, you remove all doubt.

If you really are guilty and you confess, you have let the box beat you. If, however, you are innocent and make a false confession, you will go through the rest of your life with a black stain against your name that should never have been there in the first place. And if you make a false confession and later try to recant, you will be labeled untrustworthy or unreliable, and people will have a hard time believing anything you say. Don't make the polygrapher's job easy! If he judges you deceptive, make him prove it. One study showed that an astounding 90 percent of job seekers who were rejected after being examined were tripped up not by their test results but by inadvertent admissions made during the post-test interrogation. *Never confess!*

A good interrogator will use a number of ploys to elicit a confession. He may become your "friend" and try to help you justify whatever it was you did so that it will be easier for you to "tell the truth." He will tell you that lying is difficult and tiring; telling the truth will bring about a great feeling of relief as you get the awful secret off your chest. He will try to get you to view him as a confidant, someone who really has your best interests at heart. Punishment will not be discussed initially; he just wants you to "set things right with your life."

If he senses any resistance on your part, he will move on to the next stage. He will tell you that your story doesn't square with the facts—it's just too incredible. He may try to trick you by claiming to have inside information or contradictory evidence provided by "other witnesses"; many times the witnesses and evidence are both nonexistent. Your denials and protests are cut off with a raised hand and a disappointed nod of the head. To him, your denials are all transparent and futile.

He will try to make you believe that your sole objective is to convince *him* of your innocence. He'll tell you that his opinion carries the greater weight and that if you refuse to cooperate "the game is lost." As Lykken (1981) put it, "He wants to prevent you from stubbornly repeating the same story, 'take it or leave it,' because once you have ceased to care whether he believes you, then his leverage is lost."

Don't be intimidated. Don't listen to him when he says something like, "Well just look at the charts! We got these charts from you . . . they're just your body telling us what you are too afraid to admit . . . and they're saying that you're lying!" If he tries to get away with a statement like this, you should tell him that those charts don't "say" anything. They're just a bunch of squiggly lines.

If the post-test interrogation has disintegrated to this point, there is really no more reason to stay. Unless he is a police officer and you are under arrest, he cannot prevent you from leaving. Tell him that the conversation has obviously reached an impasse that is not likely to be resolved under the present circumstances and that you are going to leave. As you make your exit, he will most likely try to trick you into staying by commenting that "deceptive persons often remove themselves from an unpleasant situation rather than face it." Don't fall for this old line. The polygrapher knows he has lost you and is just grabbing at straws.

Before you leave the office you may want to ask him if there are any provisions on his report for you to make your own statement. If there are, then you may want to say something about the questionable validity of polygraph examinations. I've included a statement that you can cut out and take with you for just such a purpose (see Appendix C). Most likely, however, you will not be allowed to make a statement on his report. You should still ask for a copy—a very reasonable request—and, if you want to rattle his cage a little bit, ask him for the name of his attorney. There is nothing like the implied threat of legal action to make someone think twice about crossing your path.

CHAPTER SEVEN

BEYOND THE POLYGRAPH: OTHER ABUSES

> "...He that hath eyes to see and ears to hear may convince himself that no mortal can keep a secret. If his lips are silent, he chatters with his fingertips; betrayal oozes out of him at every pore."
>
> —Sigmund Freud, 1905

> "Some people may see the tests as an improvement over the lie detector, but I see them as psychological rubber-hose treatments employers use to intimidate people."
>
> —Michael Tiner, legislative consultant and member of an OTA panel studying paper-and-pencil integrity tests

When the Polygraph Protection Act took effect in December 1988, many civil libertarians breathed a sigh of relief. With a single stroke of a pen, Ronald Reagan had greatly limited the extent to which private employers could invade the privacy of workers. Unfortunately, many employers felt lost without their good friend Mr. Polygraph, so they immediately set their sights on other ways to gauge the trustworthiness of both their prospective and present employees. Fortunately for them, entrepreneurs and quick-buck artists popped out of the woodwork selling all kinds of programs, equipment, courses, tapes, and seminars designed to help save the poor, victimized employer from his treacherous, thieving employees.

Today, there are no fewer than six techniques to choose from as management consultants make a

99

fortune filling the void left by the polygraph. Not surprisingly, these new methods invite the same criticisms that plagued the polygraph: invasion of privacy and lack of validity. If you are looking for a job or plan to look for one in the future, you stand a good chance of running into one of the following. Understanding what they are and how they work will give you a better chance at countering them.

KINESIOLOGY

Though actually misnomers, kinesiology and kinesic interviewing are the popular names for an examiner's attempt to judge your "true" character by interpreting telltale body movements and speech patterns. Practitioners of this art claim that the vast majority of people will give away deception through nonverbal cues even though they are successful in lying verbally. This is known as nonverbal leakage: true emotions are said to "leak out" no matter how hard the speaker tries to conceal them. A college student, for example, may say she is not nervous about a test but will bite her lower lip and blink more than usual—actions that often indicate nervousness. A young man waiting for a job interview may attempt to appear calm and casual, but he will mindlessly cross and uncross his legs, straighten his tie, touch his face, and run his fingers through his hair. As a result, he will come across looking like a nervous wreck.

The concept of leakage implies that some channels of communication leak more than others because they are less controllable. This theory is supported by several studies that have found that the body is more likely to reveal deception than the face. Tone of voice is also less controllable than facial expressions, so it may leak as well. Unfortunately, kinesic interviewing is almost impossible to detect. After all, who can say what a listener is really focusing on during a conversation? Perhaps that personnel director was really listening to your history of past accomplishments and future plans. On the other hand, perhaps he or she was only watching for discrepancies between your verbal message and your body message. Who knows? About the only way to defend against this type of lie detection is to know in advance what kinesic interviewers look for. The following list of eight major nonverbal categories should provide you with the information you need to plug up some of those pesky leaks.

Proximity

In general, the more friendly and intimate one person feels toward another, the closer he or she will stand when communicating. Friends stand closer than strangers, and people who want to seem friendly may also choose smaller distances. A good polygraph examiner will use proximity to his advantage. During the pretest interview and the test, he will maintain an appropriate distance; not being your friend, he will not try to crowd your personal space. However, if he believes your charts indicate deceptiveness, he will move in very close during the post-test interrogation. He knows that this sudden change in proximity will add to your anxiety, and he hopes that the additional pressure will finally force you to make a confession. Don't cave in. If he moves his chair close to yours, just lean back and try to act as though it does not bother you. He may be invading your personal space, but you can't let that cause you to lose self-control. If you lean back and act as if his invasion doesn't bother you, he will eventually move away and try something else.

Orientation

The angle at which you sit or stand in relation to

another person can vary from head-on to side-by-side. Although orientation can vary with different situations, different cultures, and different sexes, those who are in a cooperative situation or who are close friends tend to adopt a side-by-side position, whereas people in a bargaining position tend to choose head-on positions. A polygraph examiner will most likely confront you with a head-on position during the post-test interrogation. Your goal should be to mirror his orientation. You can still lean back in your chair while maintaining the head-on orientation, but don't shift your position in the chair so that you present the side of your body to the examiner. This is usually interpreted as an unconscious attempt at deception (i.e., you are using your body as a shield to protect against the examiner's "frontal attack").

Research has found that there are many ways a person can position his or her body to denote affiliation with others, as well as relative social status. One researcher, for example, has suggested that when people sit facing us directly or leaning in our direction and nod in agreement to what we say, we tend to interpret this to mean they like us. In contrast, we seem to interpret the following actions as signs that people do not like us: sitting so as to avoid facing us directly, leaning away from us, looking at the ceiling or floor while talking, and shaking the head in disagreement with what we are saying.

With respect to social status, it has been found that asymmetrical placement of the limbs, a sideways lean or reclining position, and relaxation of the hands or neck are behaviors that denote a higher-class communicator relating to a lower-class listener. The lower-class listener, by contrast, will usually adopt a rigid and uncomfortable (though dignified) posture. Think, for example, of a corporate CEO reclining in a leather desk chair and issuing orders to his staff. He is relaxed and comfortable; they are probably standing at attention and focusing intently on every word.

Two postural cues that are interpreted by kinesic interviewers as signs of guilt or deception are leaning toward the door of the examination room and slumping in your chair. Both should be avoided. The first denotes a desire to remove yourself from the stressful surroundings; the second is thought to indicate a desire to curl up and protect yourself from any incoming stimuli.

Head Movements

Head movements, especially nods, most often function as reinforcers to speech. For example, if you are speaking and someone is nodding his or her head up and down, you will tend to interpret that as acknowledgment or approval and continue to speak. Very rapid nods, however, indicate that the listener wants you to finish up what you are saying so he or she can speak. The affirmative quality of a nod is often used in lie detection. Many people will, for example, respond with an exaggerated "No!" when confronted with an unpleasant accusation. The head will first tilt upward and then, when the word "no" is spoken, it will rapidly tilt down to (or just below) the original position. This is interpreted as an affirmative nod that contradicts the verbal "no" message. Deception is therefore inferred. Similarly, a person who slumps his head downward (a half nod?) while he says no or just after he says no is also seen as deceptive. The same holds true for people who say no and then look away.

Facial Expressions

The face is one of the most useful communication areas. During conversations, a listener will usually provide continuous commentary on the speech of another through facial expressions. At the same time, a speaker makes facial expressions that indicate whether what is being said is supposed to be funny, important, serious, and so on. Although you might expect the face to be a reliable indicator of deception, that is not the case. Because we develop considerable control over our facial expressions as we mature, an examiner can never be sure whether an expression presented is inadvertent or ingeniously calculated. For example, some people smile when they tell a lie. Others maintain a placid expression. However, neither pupil size or perspiration can be controlled adequately when anxiety is present, so these weigh heavily in an examiner's opinion of your veracity. (It is rumored that Yasir Arafat is such a firm believer in pupil size as an indicator of deception that he never removes his sunglasses while conversing with others—even indoors.)

Despite studies showing the ineffectiveness of facial expressions for the successful detection of deception, kinesic interviewers have compiled a substantial list of "reliable" deception indicators, including: smiling nervously, shutting your eyes or looking away after a denial, flaring the nostrils, raising the eyebrows, tightening or pursing the lips, losing color in the face, denying an accusation with a look ("Who, me?"), or denying an accusation and looking intently at the examiner.

The study of gestures moved from the lab to the general public a long time ago. In recent years, many books have been published that practically guarantee that you can tell exactly what others are thinking or interpret what they are saying by observing their body movements. An open palm is said to imply an invitation; crossed legs are defensive, and so on. No one has come up with a reliable dictionary of gestures, however, because their meaning depends on such things as the context of the communication, the person making the gesture, the culture of the person, and probably a lot of other factors as well.

Be that as it may, supporters of applied kinesics have constructed voluminous lists of so-called deceptive gestures. In fact, just about any gesture you can think of has, at one time or another, been labeled an indicator of deception: crossing your legs, rubbing your legs, crossing your arms, touching or rubbing your nose or chin, touching or cleaning your glasses, grooming (wiping your nose, touching or playing with your hair, fidgeting with your shirt buttons, straightening your tie, winding your watch), pinching your nose, covering your nose or mouth with your hand, moving your hands about (especially as if to wave off statements), holding your chin, touching your lips, licking or smacking your lips, rubbing or scratching your head or neck, tapping your fingers or toes, bouncing or swinging your legs, gulping or complaining of a dry mouth, and, of course, grasping the arms of a chair so hard as to produce white knuckles.

Gazing

During a normal two-party conversation, people tend to look at each other for periods of one to ten seconds. If the conversation is unimportant or simply uninteresting, the participants may spend as much as 75 percent of the time not looking at each other, but at their surroundings. If, on the other hand, the conversation is important or interesting, the percentage of time spent looking away may drop to 25 percent. People look about twice as much when they are listening as when they are talking. Investigations of the gaze phenomena have shown that gazes serve four major functions: 1) regulating the flow of conversation, 2) monitoring feedback, 3) expressing emotions, and 4) communicating the nature of the interpersonal relationship.

At the very minimum, gaze indicates interest or

lack of it. For example, an otherwise casual conversation can become an expression of romantic interest if one of the speakers maintains steady eye contact. Conversely, avoiding or breaking the contact is usually a sign that the person is not interested. Indeed, when someone does not make eye contact during a conversation, we tend to interpret this as an indication that he or she is not really involved. No matter how attentively someone answers questions, nods at appropriate times, and carries on the conversation, the lack of eye contact means he or she is not really interested in what we are saying. But there are exceptions to this rule.

Someone who is conveying bad news or is saying something painful may avoid eye contact. Lack of eye contact can also mean that the person is frightened or shy. Likewise, when people have feelings they are embarrassed about, they usually do not like to be the focus of a direct gaze. Eye contact can also be interpreted as a threat.

There is conflicting information concerning how gazes will be interpreted from a lie detection perspective. Some say you should not try to stare too long at your examiner; others say breaking eye contact is more damaging. A frightened look characterized by continually darting your eyes about your surroundings is said to indicate guilt, as is blinking or being "shifty-eyed." Staring at the ceiling, staring at the floor, or looking "through" the examiner are also commonly characterized as indicating deception.

Paralanguage
Variations in speech qualities, distinct from the actual verbal content, are called paralanguage and can carry a great deal of meaning. Pitch, loudness, rhythm, inflections, and hesitations all convey important information. For some people, a pause may be for

emphasis, for others it may mean uncertainty. Higher pitch may mean excitement, distress, anger, fear, or surprise; a low pitch can convey pleasantness, boredom, or sadness. Loudness can mean anger, emphasis, or excitement; talking softly may make a listener think you are unsure, embarrassed, or shy. Interpreting these characteristics of language seems to be the newest rage in the lie detection industry.

Several studies have indicated that the pitch of the voice is higher when someone is lying. This difference is usually extremely small, but recently developed electronic voice analyzers are supposed to be able to measure these fluctuations and provide "accurate determinations" of truth or deception. There is also speculation that deceit can be uncovered by paying careful attention to the patterns of a person's speech. Some say that an individual who pauses for a long time before answering a question must be trying to deceive (this inference is even more likely to be made if we are already suspicious of a person's motives). Other speech patterns said to indicate deception are: using shorter sentences, making more speech errors, and replying with more nervous, less serious answers. Finally, people are thought to use words differently when they lie than when they tell the truth; they are thought to make factual statements less often, make vague, sweeping statements, or leave frequent gaps in their conversation so as to avoid "giving themselves away."

One researcher believes that deceptive language lacks spontaneity. He theorizes that when you talk normally and without stress, you tend to repeat words fairly often. But when you feel a need to be careful about a statement that may be self-incriminating, your phrasing changes. The number of different words you speak increases because you choose words you wouldn't normally use. Although this method has had three unique tests (a rape trial, a murder trial, and Richard

Nixon's "Checkers" speech), there is no hard evidence to indicate that it is a reliable lie detection method.

Human Lie Detectors

Is the leakage hypothesis correct? Does the body send out unmistakable cues that point to our deceptiveness? More importantly, can these signals be deciphered accurately by kinesic interviewers, personnel directors, or police officers? So far, the answers appear to be yes, yes, and no, respectively

Studies have shown that liars do tend to send out a wide variety of clues to their deceit, but most observers do not use all of this information, and the information they do use is not used well. For one thing, most people tend to over-rely on the verbal content, which causes them to miss important information being conveyed through other channels.

Also, people have trouble distinguishing deception from general ambivalence. This was shown in a study having three groups of "senders." The first group truthfully described their positive (or negative) feelings about another person, the second group untruthfully described their positive (or negative) feelings, and the third group described their genuinely mixed feelings. When the study was completed, the researchers found that observers were not able to distinguish truthful messages about mixed feelings from deceptive messages about positive or negative feelings. These findings suggest that people may be able to distinguish true expressions of positive or negative feelings from everything else, but they are still not able to isolate deception itself without any further information—all they know is that the person does not sound wholeheartedly positive or negative.

"But wait a minute," says the lie detection industry. "This study was conducted in an artificial laboratory setting. Why don't you give lie detection a

chance in the real world?" Two researchers (Kraut &
Poe, 1980) acknowledged this criticism and set out to
conduct a scientific experiment to see if ordinary
people are any good at detecting instances of lying in
the real world.

Ordinary citizens were approached while waiting
for an airline departure in Syracuse, New York, and
asked to smuggle some contraband past an interview
with a real U.S. Customs agent. Of the people who
agreed to participate, half were asked to play the role of
"smugglers" and half were asked to serve as an
"innocent" control group. The smugglers were given
contraband, such as small pouches of white powder or
miniature cameras, and were told to hide the items
somewhere on their person. They were also told that a
$100 prize would be given to anyone who could make
it past the customs inspector without being detected.
The innocent group, by contrast, did not get any
contraband to smuggle. Hidden video cameras were set
up to capture all the smuggler/inspector interactions.
The researchers were looking for nonverbal behaviors
exhibited by the smugglers and the innocents as they
were interviewed by the customs agents.

After all the encounters were filmed, the tapes were
given to a group of judges whose task was to chronicle
all nonverbal behavior they saw. Many of the nonverbal
behaviors outlined above were noticed, including
speech peculiarities, defensive orientations and
postures, nervous gestures, strained facial expressions,
and avoidance of prolonged eye contact. Once all the
nonverbal behaviors were categorized, the tapes were
shown to a second group of judges who had to decide
whether each individual was a smuggler or not.

The findings? Surprisingly, both the smugglers and
the innocents behaved in practically the same way,
which may explain why none of the smugglers were
detained by a customs inspector. Even more surprising

was the fact that none of the members of the second panel of judges could consistently spot a smuggler—and they knew in advance that at least some of the people on the videotapes had to be smugglers! What does this say about the leakage hypothesis? Interestingly enough, the experiment did lend some support to the notion that we constantly leak information. You see, despite the fact that none of the judges could accurately detect a smuggler, they were all fairly consistent when it came to describing the cues they thought were associated with deception. In short, this study showed that human beings are not very good lie detectors, either in the lab or in the real world.

We are, however, pretty good at describing how others *ought* to behave when they are lying, but what does that prove? Well, for one thing, it proves that this is an awfully poor technique to use if you want to try to determine someone's veracity. Nonverbal cues just don't supply us with enough information to make valid determinations of truth or deception; anyone doubting this should spend an evening with a master poker player. By the next morning, you undoubtedly will have learned the costly lesson that some people will appear more cool, calm, and confident when they're bluffing (lying) than when they're holding four aces.

PSYCHOLOGICAL STRESS EVALUATORS

Various methods of lie detection have been tested over the years to augment or even replace the standard polygraph examination. At present, researchers are developing lie detection techniques based on facial temperature, pupil and retina response, brain waves, and even stomach palpitations caused by rapid breathing under stress. Another method that once held promise dealt with body odor: apparently, we all give off a distinct body odor under stress. This was abandoned when researchers realized that there were far too many body odors to classify accurately, and any distinctive odors that might be classified were easily adulterated by cologne or aftershave lotion.

The military has always been interested in new forms of interrogation and lie detection. This led two army intelligence officers to try to find the fastest and most efficient methods for detecting deception in captured prisoners. After examining the problem from several different angles, the officers hit upon a new approach: examine the characteristics of their voices. One of the officers, Lt. Col. Allan Bell, had learned that certain vibrations or "microtremors" in the voice change when a speaker is under stress. Bell decided that fluctuations in these microtremors could also alert an interrogator to possible deceptiveness, so he started designing a device sensitive enough to pick up and chart the inaudible fluctuations of these vibrations. He eventually recruited another intelligence officer, Lt. Col. Charles McQuiston, who also happened to be an army polygraph expert. Together, they left the service, founded Dektor Counterintelligence and Security, and started producing PSEs for use by the general public.

How the PSE Works

Like the polygraph, the PSE detects stress—not lying—by measuring certain psychophysiological responses in the person being questioned. While the polygraph records blood pressure, breathing, and skin conductivity, the PSE measures only the "buzzing" vibrations, or microtremors, that are part of the characteristics of a person's voice. With a tape recorder, an individual's voice is converted into electrical energy and fed into an electronic processor. The processor isolates the microtremors from the other sounds of the voice and measures the changes in electrical energy that occur during stress. A digital display converts the electrical measure of the microtremors into numerical values, and a stylus charts the fluctuations on a bar graph. The bar graph is then analyzed for so-called deceptive patterns, and the examiner classifies the individual under investigation as either deceptive or nondeceptive.

Proponents of the PSE point out a variety of advantages: it's simpler, quicker to operate, and less threatening than a polygraph because it doesn't need any wires connected to the body. What's more, it can be used covertly. Job interviews, theft interrogations, or any telephone conversation can be recorded and later run through the machine without the subject's knowledge. Naturally, critics point out that the technique is flawed, has dubious reliability and validity, and unfairly invades the privacy of individuals whose telephone conversations are surreptitiously recorded and then analyzed without their knowledge or consent.

Anecdotal Evidence

Because the vast majority of rigorously controlled scientific studies give the PSE miserable performance ratings, its proponents often rely on unsubstantiated anecdotal evidence to impress prospective buyers of the machine. Some of these "case studies" are, if nothing else, interesting examples of the PSE in action.

* A free-lance writer used one to check tapes of Lee Harvey Oswald's statements after his capture in Dallas ("I didn't shoot anybody, no sir," Oswald said) and concluded that he was innocent.
* Other investigators checked out Edward Kennedy's televised remarks after the tragedy at Chappaquidick and reported that he, too, seemed to be telling the truth.
* John Dean, Howard Hughes, Patty Hearst, and

Richard Nixon have all had various statements evaluated for their truthfulness with a PSE machine.

* The makers of the PSE have even used it to test contestants on the old TV game show, "To Tell the Truth," and claimed a suspiciously high 95-percent accuracy in spotting the liars.

* According to the August 15, 1978 issue of *National Enquirer*, three U.S. Air Force officers who flatly denied that the United States was involved in some kind of UFO cover-up were actually lying. PSE evaluations of their recorded interviews were conducted by none other than Charles McQuiston himself.

* McQuiston also reported in the October 24, 1978 issue of *National Enquirer* that "something extraordinary" happened to Carl Higdon, who claims he was abducted by a flying saucer and carried off to its native planet before being returned to Earth. According to McQuiston, "Some parts of his statements show stress, but other parts show no stress at all, indicating he's telling the truth."

* Internationally known psychic Francie Steiger claims she is in daily contact with Kihief—her guardian angel. PSE examiner Forrest Erickson confirmed her statement in the October 24, 1978 issue of *Midnight/Globe*.

* "Without a doubt [he] is telling the truth" was the statement made by Erickson on claims from another bizarre UFO case involving Mr. Charles Hickson. Hickson, you may remember, started a media frenzy in 1973 when he reported that he, along with a fellow shipyard worker, was abducted from a Pascagoula, Mississippi, swamp while fishing and given a physical examination aboard a UFO. (*UFO Report*, November, 1978.)

* Erickson also gave his endorsement to the strange case of Travis Walton, a lumberjack who

claimed to have been "zapped" by a UFO, knocked unconscious, and carried aboard the vessel, where he subsequently regained consciousness and was surrounded by "strange-looking creatures." Walton's claims were further supported by McQuiston, who concluded that "there is little, if any, possibility of a hoax involvement in telling the story." (*Fate*, October, 1978.)

Controlled Studies of the PSE

Since the army had been inadvertently instrumental in the development of the PSE, you might expect that many federal agencies would be making great use of it. That, however, is not the case. Various military and other intelligence agencies did buy and test a few voice analyzers in the early 1970s, but most of those machines have been discarded, dismantled, or destroyed. The Pentagon's National Security Agency tested the device and found it "insufficiently reliable." The U.S. Air Force Office of Special Investigations conducted sixty tests of its own and ultimately declared that the PSE was "not useful." Finally, the army commissioned a comparative study of the voice analyzers and the polygraph at Fordham University and found that the PSE achieved an accuracy rate barely equal to that of pure chance. In other words, the government doesn't believe the PSE even meets the standards of the polygraph exam, and we all know by now how unreliable polygraph exams are.

The polygraph industry was quick to point out its displeasure with PSE technology. For reasons that may have had as much to do with protecting their favored "lie detection" status as with scientific rigor, the American Polygraph Association criticized the PSE on two fronts: 1) inadequate examiner training, and 2) inadequate measures of the various "information channels."

With regard to training, the American Polygraph

Association attacked the PSE companies for allowing their students to conduct real-life exams after only *five days* of training (even the brief training given to polygraph examiners in the private sector is longer than this). The PSE companies claim five days is long enough because their machines are simpler to operate than a polygraph (true), and the results are easier to interpret (debatable). As for the second criticism, the American Polygraph Association is squarely against using the PSE as a stand-alone lie detector because it measures only one physiological response (as opposed to the polygraph's three). In a conciliatory gesture, however, the APA went on to conclude that the PSE might serve as a possible aid to a standardized polygraph exam by gauging the stress associated with the verbalization channel, thus adding another bit of information to the evaluation.

The Real Test

Despite the bickering between polygraph examiners and PSE examiners, both sides privately agree that the real worth of these devices is in their ability to produce confessions. And just like a skilled polygrapher, a skilled PSE examiner armed with his charts can get many individuals to break down and confess. As I've said before, you should never confess to anything. Once you confess, you've admitted defeat; if you don't confess, then it's just your word against his.

With that in mind, here are some pointers, gleaned from a newsletter published by the International Society of Stress Analysts, on how to interrogate a theft suspect. (Keep in mind how you would respond to this treatment and whether or not you would be tempted to confess.)

* Begin an interrogation immediately after determining that the charts point toward deception.

* Confessions are elicited more easily when you are alone with the subject in a private room.

* Don't show the charts to the subject unless his responses are "truly dramatic." Less dramatic patterns can lead to pointless arguments with the subject concerning your conclusions.

* Don't bully your suspect; become his friend. Sympathize with him and tell him of others in the same situation who felt tremendous relief upon confessing.

* Point out to the suspect any physiological indicators of deception he may be exhibiting in addition to his chart data (dry mouth, sweating, upset stomach, elevated blood pressure, red face, etc.).

* Minimize the gravity of the crime to make it easier for the suspect to confess.

* If your subject is nonemotional, appeal to his common sense. Point out the futility of lying.

* Rationalize the offense by helping your subject blame others for the crime: justify his act, blame the victim, his accomplice, his wife, parents, partner, or anyone.

It's no wonder that this type of lie detection interrogation is often called the "psychological rubber hose."

PAPER-AND-PENCIL TESTS

Paper-and-pencil measures of honesty are quickly becoming the number-one method for preemployment screening. These so-called "integrity tests" were rarely used when it was still legal to administer polygraph examinations for preemployment screening, but they are now firmly embraced by business owners and personnel directors looking for an inexpensive (and still legal) way of weeding out undesirable job candidates. Integrity tests are based on the assumption that a more forgiving attitude toward dishonesty predisposes a person to dishonest behavior.

These tests fall into two categories: overt honesty tests and broader-based personality tests. Overt honesty tests assess a person's attitude toward the problems of dishonesty in the workplace by asking, for example, for opinions about how honest or dishonest the average person is and how honest or dishonest the test taker sees himself as compared to the average person ("I believe that most people are generally honest," or "Compared to other people, I feel that I am fairly honest"). Broader-based personality tests, on the other hand, measure a broader range of traits, such as employee reliability, deviance, social conformity, loyalty, initiative, and hostility to rules.

Problems

The major flaw of these integrity tests is that in order to pass you must exhibit a punitive and authoritarian personality. If a test question asks, "Do you believe that an individual who takes a pen home from work is a thief," then you must answer "yes," because the test developers consider even these small crimes to be unacceptable. The rationale is that someone who commits or condones small crimes will progress to bigger and bigger crimes.

Another question might be: "The department store where you work has a strict policy of destroying all damaged merchandise so that they can collect the insurance for it. One day, a well-liked and reliable but financially struggling five-year employee is caught at a Dumpster removing disposable diapers from their damaged boxes so that he can take them home for his new baby girl. Should he be treated as a shoplifter?" Once again, if you want to pass this question, you have to answer "yes." The rationale is that a thief will be unlikely to recommend harsh punishment for acts he might commit himself, and he will probably also contend that most people are just as dishonest as he is.

That may be true, but what about those people who are naturally lenient and are more likely to "give the guy a break"? Are they to be less trusted employees? Will they be less productive? Less reliable? And what about people who have a cynical nature—those who don't trust their fellow man and are always looking for ulterior motives? They may truly believe that most people take things from their employers, but if they respond affirmatively to this attitude on an integrity test, then they will be penalized for being honest! Is that fair?

A second problem with these tests is that they assume that thievery is a personality trait just as "outgoing, bubbly, and friendly" are. Consequently, you cannot admit to thefts in the past (like taking home a pen) because the test developers assume that if you have stolen in the past, you will steal again in the future. Of course, this is a totally unreasonable and unprovable hypothesis. In fact, recent research seems to indicate that employee theft is probably more dependent on situational factors (e.g., easy opportunity, resentment or anger toward employer, special need for the item) than enduring personality traits that can be measured by a test. In other words, past behavior is a poor predictor of future behavior, and if a company wants to reduce the amount of employee theft, it should spend its money on measures that will make it harder for an employee to steal rather than on some test developed to assess personality traits.

Other problems with integrity tests have to do with improper construction and, again, poor examiner training. In regard to the former, some psychologists or personnel directors simply go to an existing personality test, remove the sections that apply to social dysfunction or social pathology and then use this as an "honesty test." The problem with this practice is that the developer of the original personality inventory never intended it to be pulled apart and used as some sort of half-baked honesty test—all his reliability and validity studies guaranteeing the usefulness of the test are rendered worthless when someone comes along and uses only the parts of the test that seem to measure a particular trait.

Secondly, these tests are often sold to organizations that have no one properly trained to administer, score, and interpret them. As any professional psychometrician (a psychologist who specializes in testing) will tell you, there is a big difference between administering and scoring a psychological test and administering and scoring a fourth-grade spelling test. Unfortunately, many companies don't realize (or don't care) that many variables must be controlled to get an accurate score on a psychological test. This may be one reason these integrity tests produce such a large number of false positives (those who are incorrectly labeled as dishonest). Studies have shown that 40 to 60 percent of all test takers fail.

Sample Test

Would you like to see how you might fare on an honesty test? Try the five questions below. Answer truthfully.

1) An employer discovers that a trusted, long-term employee has been taking home one or two dollars a week from the "coffee fund." Should the employer have him arrested?

Yes / No

2) How should an employee caught smoking marijuana on the job be handled?

Ignored / Warned / Suspended / Fired / Arrested

3) What percentage of your friends would you rate as really honest?

95% / 80% / 50% / 20% / 10% or less

4) What percentage of employees do you believe takes small things from employers from time to time?

95% / 80% / 50% / 20% / 10% or less

5) What percentage of people do you believe cheats on income taxes?

95% / 80% / 50% / 20% / 10% or less

How do you think you did? Well, if you answered "Yes," "Arrested," "95%," "10% or less," and "10% or less," you stand a good chance of passing one of these tests. If your answers were different, you may be in trouble. Remember, to pass a test like this you must never admit to *anything*. As Dr. Philip Ash, research director for the Reid organization explained: "Incredible as it may seem, applicants in significant numbers do admit to practically every crime in the books."

You must also remember to answer all the questions like an ultraconservative, extreme right-winger would: taking something (no matter how small) is always a crime, people who take things are criminals, and criminals should be arrested and locked up for as long as possible. Adopting this type of attitude is the safest way to pass a so-called integrity test.

GRAPHOLOGY

Graphology is one of the oldest and least convincing methods of lie detection used. It dates back hundreds of years, with the actual term "graphology" having been coined by the French cleric Michon around 1871. Interest in graphological techniques has continued unabated in this century, and it is easy to go into any large bookstore and find half a dozen books claiming to possess all the secrets of handwriting analysis. There is even computer software now on the market that will produce a report detailing a person's "social behavior; intellectual style; personality traits; and physical, emotional, and material drives." All you do is key in the answers to sixty questions regarding a handwriting sample's characteristics. To help you along, the software includes twenty-eight handwriting samples so you can check up on such luminaries as Ronald Reagan, Elizabeth Taylor, Edgar Allan Poe, and Queen Elizabeth II.

Graphology as an employment tool initially developed its largest following in Europe, particularly France, where it is still practically impossible to be considered for a job unless you submit a sample of your handwriting for analysis. During the 1980s, graphology made its way into the U.S. business community, where today it is said to be used by five to ten thousand companies (although the numbers are difficult to substantiate because many companies, fearing ostracism by their competitors or clients, will not acknowledge that they rely on this hocus-pocus in making personnel decisions).

Now that the majority of preemployment polygraph exams are illegal, the reliance upon graphology is almost certain to increase. Some critics argue that these businesses are trading one form of witchcraft for another, but that hasn't stopped the International Graphoanalysis Society in Chicago from churning out more than ten thousand "accredited" graphoanalysts, with another two thousand on the way. Graduates of its correspondence course—the only one of its kind in the United States—earn the title "certified graphoanalyst" after eighteen months of study and "master graphoanalyst" after thirty-six months. Upon completion of the coursework, these certified analysts are free to charge from thirty dollars to three hundred dollars per analysis, depending on the type of information the client desires.

What do graphoanalysts look for? Unfortunately, that is not a simple question to answer because there are several competing schools of graphology, each with its own history, approach, and theory. In fact, if you look through two or three books on the subject of handwriting analysis, you will notice there is little agreement on which factors are the most important. More disturbing is the fact that these books give totally different interpretations for the same factors.

Dozens of these so-called personality indicators may be analyzed (depending on which school you believe), but some of the most common ones are: size of writing; percentage of page used; slant of letters; height of letters; width of letters; relative consistency of slant, height, and width of letters throughout a sample; connectedness of letters within words; pressure on the page; spacing of words; regularity of crossed *t's* and dotted *i's*; where the *t's* and *i's* are crossed and dotted; and whether the letters loop above or below the line. Some analysts also measure the speed of a person's handwriting. How is an analysis of all these factors carried out? Once again, interpretations vary, but some of the possibilities include:

* *Dotting i's and crossing t's.* Dots that look more like lines than dots are said to indicate anger. Dots to the left of the *i* show procrastination. Forgetting to dot the *i* shows inattentiveness, as does leaving the bar off the *t*. If the bar is above the *t*, the person is said to have high or "visionary" goals. The bar at the top of the *t* means the person has distant goals, the middle of the *t* means practical goals, and low on the *t* means low or no goals.

* *Rounding m's and n's.* A rounded *m* or *n* is said to mean a person accumulates information and then makes

a decision. A more pointed *m* or *n*, one that looks like an inverted *v*, may indicate keen comprehension.

* *Height of letter stems.* The farther into the "upper zone" the stems go, the more developed the imagination and creativity. Lower-zone stems indicate sensual perception, unconscious drives, and biological needs. Long *g* and *y* stems, for example, may show an unconscious but strong sense of materialism.

* *Slant of letters.* Straight letters (depending on who you believe) are said to show objectivity or introvertedness. Letters that slant to the left show self-absorption, and letters that slant to the right show emotional sensitivity (or logic).

* *Pressure.* Heavy pressure is said to indicate anger or stubbornness; light pressure denotes insecurity. Some critics of graphology suggest that you use a felt-tip pen when preparing your handwriting sample so that the "pressure" factor is rendered useless.

* *Speed.* The speed with which you complete your sample is used by some analysts as a measure of how natural, spontaneous, and genuine you are.

* *Consistency of height and slant.* A consistent pattern of letter height and slant is said to indicate balance and self-control in your life. Irregular patterns indicate that you are not in full control and that you let the events of your life overwhelm you.

At first glance, these interpretations, compiled from several books and a certified graphoanalyst, may seem silly. After all, does it really take eighteen months of training to interpret leaving the bar off the *t* as a sign of inattentiveness? I don't think so. But I also don't think that graphology should be brushed off as some sort of harmless parlor game. Consider the following.

The president of an Atlanta-area business dealing with photocopying equipment reported in the January 18, 1989 issue of *Atlanta Journal* that, based on a graphoanalyst's advice, he has hired six good employees and screened out eighteen others with whom he was impressed initially. How do you think those eighteen people would feel if they knew they were screened out because a so-called expert didn't like the way they crossed their *t's* and dotted their *i's*? How would you feel? I would be mad as hell. But graphoanalysts will argue that they are trained professionals using tried-and-true scientific principles. Unfortunately for them, the mainstream scientific community does not agree, as the following sampling of conclusions from some controlled scientific studies of graphology demonstrates.

* Ben-Shakhar, Bar-Hillel, Bilin, and Flug (1986): "The graphologists did not perform significantly better than a chance model."
* Furnham and Gunter (1987): ". . . the theoretical basis of the method appears weak, nonexplicit, and nonparsimonious."
* Lester, McLaughlin, and Nosal (1977): "No evidence was found for the validity of the graphological signs."
* Rosenthal and Lines (1978): "Thus the results did not support the claim that the three handwriting measures were valid indices of extraversion."
* Vestewig, Santee, and Moss (1976): "It was concluded that the analyst could not accurately predict personality from handwriting."

Despite the negative findings, graphology continues to flourish because overworked, stressed-out managers are constantly under the gun to find reliable job candidates who won't rob the company blind. And since mainstream psychologists have yet to produce a simple and 100-percent predictive measure of personality, these managers feel forced to turn to the graphoanalysts.

Interestingly, most graphologists will not attempt to determine the sex of the writer from a handwriting sample, even though the average American citizen has been shown to succeed in this task about 70 percent of the time. (To protect themselves from being brought up on discrimination charges, graphologists typically don't receive personal information, such as age or sex, about the applicant.) They explain their reluctance to predict sex by insisting that handwriting reveals psychological, not biological, characteristics. This sounds like a cop-out to me. I find it difficult to believe that these analysts cannot make a simple prediction of sex, even though they will not hesitate to make absolute predictions about such abstract constructs as a person's belief system, motives, and personality. Perhaps they don't want to make judgments about gender because it could too easily be used as a gauge of their abilities. After all, how much faith would you put in a three-page personality profile if the graphoanalyst couldn't even determine the sex of the applicant?

RECENT DEVELOPMENTS

One of the great things about the United States is that entrepreneurship is openly encouraged by the government through tax breaks, low-interest loans, and the like. Many times, the success or failure of a business depends not on the quality of the product, but rather on the product's ability to fill a need—often expressed as "being in the right place at the right time." Such is the case with the lie detection industry. The banning of polygraph exams for most pre-employment screening left a void in the marketplace, and entrepreneurs have been quick to provide alternative methods of personnel selection that circumvent the Polygraph Protection Act.

The Quick Phone Test
Although Georgia-based TeleScreen was founded

long before the passage of the Polygraph Protection Act, the company realized a 100-percent increase in revenues in the two months prior to the ban on polygraph testing, and it expects to see increased revenues throughout the 1990s because this system can now be marketed as a legal alternative to the polygraph test. In TeleScreen's test, a job applicant telephones a computer and responds to 150 questions asked by a recorded voice. The applicant has only three seconds to respond to each question by pressing buttons for "yes," "no," or "not applicable." According to the test's creator, the quick response time prohibits the applicant from reviewing and possibly changing his answers (which a paper-and-pencil honesty test would allow) and thus promotes truthfulness.

At twelve to twenty dollars an interview, Tele-Screen hopes to convince its prospective clients that it is both a legal and cost-effective alternative to standard polygraph testing. What's more, the duration of a TeleScreen interview is less than ten minutes, and the applicant doesn't have to be wired to a machine, making the procedure less stressful than a polygraph exam. On the negative side, there is absolutely no evidence that a quick response time automatically compels people to tell the truth. Also, applicants who take the test using a phone with touch keys mounted in the handset would have to listen to the question, remove the handset from his ear, find the right touch key, punch it in, and return the handset to his ear, all in the allotted three seconds. Needless to say, all this fumbling around could cause some applicants to be penalized unfairly.

Despite these drawbacks, TeleScreen aggressively markets not only its testing service, but also a stand-alone system you can purchase for your own place of business. The complete systems are priced from ten thousand to fifty thousand dollars. Add to this a four-dollar software licensing fee for each interview once the system is installed. (These costs are, of course, deductible as business expenses.) As with many other forms of lie detection, it is difficult to establish an accurate estimate of its validity. Company accuracy claims of 95 percent are suspiciously high and should be taken with a grain of salt.

Brain Wave Analysis

This technique is scheduled to be on the market in 1992 and may already be in use in limited areas. Quite simply, it is purported to be a "polygraph of the mind." Instead of measuring the physical expressions of emotion—pulse rate, sweating, blood pressure, and breathing rate—it measures actual brain wave activity through electrodes attached to the scalp. These signals are then amplified and fed into a computer, which coordinates the information and displays it on a video screen.

The theory behind this technique is that normal brain wave activity will break into a special kind of trough called P3 wave whenever an individual is presented with sensory information that has a special meaning for him. University tests on students, for example, have used words like "cheating" or "cocaine" to see if they cause a shift into the P3 wave, the implication being that the students who exhibit such a shift might be involved in these particular activities. Obviously, this technique suffers from the same drawbacks as the standard polygraph. Most damaging is the assumption that any word possessing enough of the requisite "personal meaning" factor to cause a shift to the P3 wave automatically incriminates the person being tested.

Let's look at the word "cocaine," for example. Perhaps you exhibit P3 waves at this word because you grew up in a drug-infested neighborhood and barely survived all the turf wars and random acts of violence associated with such areas. You may have never used cocaine in your life, but I would bet you that the word "cocaine" has a special meaning for you. Should you now be accused of using cocaine because you grew up in a bad neighborhood? I don't think so, and I don't think brain wave analysis has sufficient safeguards built in to protect you in such situations as these.

Brain wave lie detectors are still in the planning stages, and the basic system, if completed, is expected to cost ten times as much as a standard polygraph. The complexity of the system would also require much more training than is generally provided for the typical polygraph examiner. If past experience with the polygraph and psychological stress evaluator is any indication, however, I am afraid that someone will eventually come along and make the brain wave analyzer cheaper, lower the standards for training, and make a fortune. At the same time, thousands of people will be unfairly discriminated against simply because they didn't react according to some examiner's preconceived notion of normalcy.

CONCLUSION

What does the future hold for polygraph/integrity testing? I can foresee three possible scenarios:

1) An enlightened bureaucracy realizes the folly of veracity testing and quickly passes legislation to prevent it. (Not likely.)

2) An outraged public grows tired of lie detection abuses and forces Congress to act. (Again, not very likely.)

3) Things stay pretty much the same. (Very likely.)

It is a sad fact that we have become a nation of noncritical thinkers. By and large, we don't question the claims we read in the newspapers or see on TV because we assume they must be true. In short, we often choose to take things at face value when a little skepticism is in order. Consider the following, for example.

* Graphologists won't make judgments about the sex of a person based on a handwriting sample. Why not? I think it's a fair question, and one that should be answered before we let the graphologist delve into more abstract components of our personality.

* Polygraphers make the assumption that someone who lies must become physiologically aroused. Why? Where is their proof?

* Proponents of the Quick Phone Test assume that a three-second response time promotes truthfulness. Is it their claim that it takes more cognitive processing to lie than to tell the truth? Can they prove this?

Because we don't require the lie detection industry to answer tough questions like these, we have given tacit approval to its operations. I believe this has gone on long enough.

Unfortunately, the truth merchants have grown to the point that they now enjoy considerable financial and political clout. We may not be able to put them out of business, but we can certainly make their jobs more difficult. I hope that this book will help you to do just that.

Just remember, the outcome of an integrity test is very much determined by how well you perform under pressure. So good luck, and remember to practice, practice, practice.

POLYGRAPH DO'S AND DON'TS

IF YOU ARE ASKED TO TAKE A POLYGRAPH EXAM . . .

DO learn your legal rights. As of this writing, at least eighteen states and the District of Columbia have statutes that either prohibit employers from requesting or requiring tests or forbid mandatory testing.

DO contact your union representative if you are covered by a labor contract. You may have some protection or recourse through grievance or arbitration procedures.

DO discuss the matter with fellow employees. On occasion, groups of workers have balked and their employers have backed down.

DO tell your employer that polygraph tests can be inaccurate and that the mainstream scientific community has serious concerns about their validity.

DO contact your local office of the American Civil Liberties Union (ACLU) or legal aid society. They can tell you what your legal rights are concerning polygraph testing.

DON'T be afraid to speak up for your rights.

DON'T expect to be treated fairly. Remember, polygraph examiners are paid to find the guilty—not to clear the innocent.

IF YOU AGREE TO TAKE THE EXAM . . .

DO study this book. You want to go into the exam with a thorough knowledge of what will go on inside that room.

DO practice identifying your question categories. You stand a much greater chance of failing if you can't differentiate between control questions and relevant questions.

DO practice your countermeasures. Practice makes perfect.

DO dress nicely for the test. If you show up looking like a bum, expect to be treated like a bum.

DO bring something to read. You never know who may be watching while you sit in the waiting room.

DO be on time! "Show up late, you've cast your fate."

DO be friendly. Make a good first impression.

DO express confidence that the test will clear you.

DON'T be sarcastic. Making fun of the examiner or the test itself will not score you any points.

DON'T be belligerent or argue with the examiner about polygraph validity. You want the examiner to believe that you are a willing and enthusiastic participant.

DON'T fidget. It makes you look guilty.

DON'T be shifty-eyed. That *really* makes you look guilty.

DON'T complain about a dry mouth. An examiner

will interpret this as fear over being found out and may press you even harder during the test or the post-test interrogation.

DON'T sign away any legal rights. An examiner will pressure you to do this, but don't cave in. He's just trying to protect himself, not you.

IF YOU THINK YOU'VE FAILED THE EXAM . . .

DO ask to see the test report. Also ask if you can make a statement on the report (see Appendix C).

DO ask for a second opinion. This does not mean getting the examiner's colleague to reinterpret your present chart. This means going to an entirely different polygrapher and getting him to run a whole new test.

DON'T volunteer any information and **DON'T** admit to anything. One study showed that 90 percent of the job applicants who were rejected after being examined were tripped up by their own admissions, not by the test results.

DON'T be intimidated. If you're fired, harassed, or otherwise abused because of a lie detector test, see a lawyer. The American Polygraph Association and numerous authorities say that polygraph test results should never be the sole basis for termination.

APPENDIX B

POLYGRAPHERS' FAVORITE VERBAL PLOYS

▼▼▼▼▼

Many polygraphers will use whatever means are necessary to get you to confess. One of their favorite tricks is to confuse you or misdirect your attention in an attempt to get you to see things their way. The following statements have all been used during actual polygraph examinations. Notice how they are designed to either set you up during a pretest interview or wear you down during a post-test interrogation. Following each statement is the thought process you must use to fight this kind of intimidation. Study these.

1) *"The machine says you're lying."* The machine says no such thing. It is just a bunch of squiggly lines. He's the one who is saying that I'm lying, and I don't put much faith in his opinions.

2) *"Remember, these exams*

are 95-percent accurate." Totally false. There has never been a properly controlled study resulting in accuracy rates that high.

3) *"I've been doing this a long time, and I know all the tricks."* He's putting me on the defensive and subtly warning me not to try anything. Don't believe this statement—studies have shown that even experienced examiners catch only the most blatant countermeasure attempts.

4) *"I'd stake my career on this machine."* Of course he would. Without it, he wouldn't have a career.

5) *"All the scientific evidence says that polygraph exams are reliable and valid."* A total falsehood. What the scientific evidence shows is that these exams are unpredictable at best, and I sure wouldn't want my fate trusted to one of them. If they are so reliable, why aren't they admissible in court?

6) *"I'm not out to get you."* Not true. The examiner is always trying to "get" someone, or he wouldn't be in business for very long. Remember, if he doesn't find someone guilty, he probably won't get any more business from that company or sponsor. Do you think he wants to risk that?

7) *"I'm a former police officer, and I've had ____ years of training and experience."* So what? The fact that he's a former police officer doesn't make him any more qualified to give polygraph exams than a former butcher, cab driver, or window washer.

8) *"If you're innocent, you've got nothing to worry about."* To prepare for this one, reread Chapter 2.

9) *"I can tell five minutes after I meet someone whether he is guilty or not."* The unmistakable sign of an arrogant examiner. If he's really that good, what does he need the machine for?

10) *"Countermeasures don't work."* Maybe he'd like to think so, but the truth is that there are

documented cases of people who have used countermeasures to beat an exam who have subsequently confessed or have been otherwise found guilty of the crime being investigated.

11) *"I'm going to have to tell your employer that you're the strongest candidate so far."* The ultimate in intimidation. The only reason he is sharing this opinion with me is because he wants me to confess. This is one of the oldest tricks in the book. Don't fall for it.

12) *"Remember, the machine doesn't lie"* or *"The machine never makes mistakes."* Of course it doesn't. It's just a machine that charts respiration, perspiration, and heart rate. He's the one I'm worried about making mistakes.

13) *"When you lie, you show definite signs of physiological arousal."* This has never been proven. When you're anxious, you show definite signs of physiological arousal, but being anxious and telling a lie are two entirely different things.

14) *"My interpretations are totally objective."* Like "military intelligence" and "jumbo shrimp," objective interpretation is an oxymoron. No human opinion can be totally objective, because the definition of objectivity requires that it be free of all personal bias or prejudice. Humans can only make subjective interpretations.

15) *"This test is for your benefit, not your harm."* What a joke. The test is for the employer's benefit, and the polygrapher usually doesn't care who gets harmed along the way.

16) *"I'll be watching for countermeasures, and I can almost always spot them."* Another statement designed to put me on the defensive. Think about this. How does he know he almost always spots countermeasures being used? Maybe he only spots the clumsy ones. The good ones, the ones that pass, may be slipping right by him. He has no way of knowing.

17) *"This machine can't be beat."* True, but an examiner can be beat.

18) *"We know you did it. Why don't you just confess and get it off your chest?"* Here, the examiner is trying to trick me into believing that he has some kind of inside information. This type of ploy works surprisingly often during post-test interrogations.

Do not fall for it.

19) *"Who are you trying to protect?"* This is one of those devious questions on the order of, "Do you still beat your wife?" There is no good way to answer it. If I answer that I'm not trying to protect anyone, the examiner will infer that I'm trying to protect myself. If, on the other hand, I admit that I am trying to protect someone, the examiner has won. He hasn't yet extracted a confession, but he's well on his way.

20) *"We could run this test one hundred more times, and I would still get the same results."* Time to ask to get a second opinion from another examiner. People who make statements like this have let their egos get the best of them. No one is able to reason with them because they think they're always right.

POLYGRAPH VALIDITY STATEMENTS

Office of Technology Assessment (OTA), an investigative arm of Congress, mandated to review and evaluate the advancements of and potential problems with current technology, has issued the following conclusions with respect to polygraph testing:

". . . no overall measure or single statistic of polygraph validity can be established based on available scientific evidence. Further, regardless of whether polygraph testing is used in specific incident investigations or personnel screening, OTA concluded that polygraph accuracy may be affected by a number of factors: examiner training, orientation, and experience; examinee characteristics such as emotional stability and intelligence; and, in particular, the use of countermeasures and the willingness of the examinee to be tested. In addition, the basic theory (or theories) of how the polygraph test actually works has been only minimally developed and researched.

In sum, OTA concluded that there is at present only limited scientific evidence for establishing the validity of polygraph testing. Even where the evidence seems to indicate that polygraph testing detects deceptive subjects better than chance (when using the control question technique in specific incident criminal investigations), significant error rates are possible, and examiner and examinee differences and the use of countermeasures may further affect validity."

CUT OUT AND SAVE!

GLOSSARY

anecdotal evidence: Uncontrolled and unsystematic observations. If you wear a particular shirt to a math test because you have always done well in the past while wearing it, you are basing your shirt choice on anecdotal evidence.

Backster school: A major polygraph training facility which teaches (among other things) that decisions of truth or deception must be made entirely on the data contained in the polygraph charts.

baseline: The readings on a polygraph chart that form a point of comparison for the physiological responses to the polygraph questions.

biofeedback: The control of internal processes such as heart rate, brain waves, or the galvanic skin response (GSR) through behavioral conditioning.

bogus pipeline: A procedure

whereby subjects are attached, via skin electrodes, to an imposing collection of electronic gadgetry so as to elicit truthful attitudes in situations where social desirability (i.e., subjects' desire to express socially acceptable opinions) may mask actual attitudes. The gadgetry is really junk, and the purpose of the procedure is to convince subjects that their actual attitudes are detectable.

construct validity: A type of validity determined by the extent to which the items making up a test are true measures of the construct or process being tested. In other words, the extent to which a test measures what it is supposed to measure.

control question: A type of polygraph question designed to be more arousing for nondeceptive subjects and less arousing for deceptive subjects than the relevant questions.

Control Question Technique (CQT): A polygraph testing technique that incorporates control questions.

countermeasures: Deliberate techniques used by subjects to avoid detection during a polygraph examination.

electrodermal response (EDR): A physiological measure that has been shown to be related to psychological arousal. It is measured as the electrical resistance of the skin through the use of electrodes attached to the fingertips.

false negative: An erroneous conclusion that an individual is not being deceptive when he or she actually is.

false positive: An erroneous conclusion that a person is being deceptive when he or she is actually being truthful.

field study: An experimental study using actual polygraph data from trained polygraph examiners.

galvanic skin response (GSR): See electrodermal response.

generalizability: The extent to which results of laboratory experiments can be applied to "real world" situations.

global scoring technique: A scoring procedure that uses behavioral symptoms, case facts, and other extraneous bits of information in conjunction with the actual polygraph chart data to make an overall determination of a subject's veracity.

Guilty Knowledge Technique (GKT): A polygraph testing technique that does not detect lying per se but attempts to detect whether a suspect has information about a crime that only a guilty person would have.

halo effect: The tendency to give individuals a rating or evaluation that is too high or too low overall on the basis of one outstanding trait.

hot question: A polygraph question that elicits a pronounced physiological response from a subject.

hypnosis: A sleeplike state induced artificially and characterized by greatly heightened suggestibility. Can be used as a cognitive countermeasure on a polygraph exam.

inconclusive: Outcome of an examination in which it cannot be determined from the subject's responses whether he or she is being deceptive.

irrelevant questions: Neutral questions designed to assess the subject's baseline physiological response to questioning and to provide a rest between relevant questions.

kinetic information: Gestures, expressive movements, posture, and tension patterns used in making judgments about persons.

laboratory study: An experiment conducted in a controlled environment in which the experimenter controls and manipulates all the experimental variables.

lie response: A presumed set of overt behaviors that are thought to be indicative of deception.

orienting response: An initial elevated response that occurs when a subject is presented with any new stimulus (for example, the first question on a polygraph exam will usually evoke an elevated orienting response).

paralanguage: Information conveyed by variations in speech other than actual words and syntax, such as pitch, loudness, hesitations, and so on.

physiological arousal: Responses related to increases in anxiety. Those measured in polygraph examinations include electrodermal response, blood pressure, and respiration rate.

pneumatic chair: A counter-countermeasure used by polygraphers to detect any extraneous physical movements that may indicate a physical counter-measure in use. It is usually a cushioned armchair fitted with strain gauges in the seat, arms, and back.

pneumographs: Rubber tubes placed around a subject's chest and abdomen to measure respiration.

post-test interrogation: The time period following the actual polygraph examination during which the examiner discusses the test with the subject and attempts to elicit a confession.

preemployment screening: The use of polygraph testing to assess the character of employee applicants.

pressure chair: See pneumatic chair.

pretest interview: The first portion of the polygraph testing procedure during which subjects are informed about the examination as well as their legal rights. In some pretest interviews, examiners also make observations about subjects' behavior to assist in their overall conclusions.

psychological separation: A presumed ability on the part of the subject to perceive relevant questions differently from "inclusive" control questions (that is, control questions whose content is of the same general nature as the crime under investigation).

Reid school: A major polygraph training facility that teaches (among other things) that conclusions of truth or deception should be based on behavioral symptoms, case facts, and other extraneous bits of information in addition to the data provided in the actual polygraph charts. This is known as a global scoring technique.

relevant questions: Polygraph questions about the topic or topics under investigation.

Relevant/Irrelevant Technique (R/I): A polygraph testing technique that utilizes two types of questions—relevant questions intended to assess a subject's degree of anxiety across a variety of subject areas and irrelevant (neutral) questions intended to assess the subject's baseline response.

reliability: The degree to which a test yields repeatable results. Also refers to the consistency with which similarly trained examiners give consistent scores to the same chart data.

sphygmomanometer: Blood pressure cuff used to assess heart rate.

stimulation test: A number or card test given to the subject before the actual test begins or after the first round of questions. Usually explained to the subject as a means of "calibrating" the machine; in reality, the stim test is designed to reassure truthful subjects of the machine's validity and provoke anxiety in deceptive subjects.

validity: A measure of the extent to which an observed situation reflects the "true" situation.